TOMORROW'S WORLD

ANIMAL INTELLIGENCE UNLEASHED

I0878981

ANIMAL INTELLIGENCE UNLEASHED

Written by
Jill Russo

Illustrated by
Eszter Szepvolgyi

First published in 2025 by Hungry Tomato Ltd, F15, Old Bakery Studios, Blewetts Wharf, Malpas Road, Truro, Cornwall, TR1 1QH, UK.

Editor: Millie Burdett
Graphic Designer: Amy Harvey
Cover Designers: Amy Harvey and Sam Fleetwood
Consultants: Li Yimeng and Liu Haiming

With thanks to Nicola Carthy

Copyright © 2025 Hungry Tomato Ltd and China Children's Press & Publication Group Co., Ltd

No part of this publication may be reproduced, stored in a retrieval system, or transmitted in any form or by any means, electronic, mechanical, photocopying, recording, or otherwise, without prior written permission of the copyright owner.

A CIP catalog record for this book is available from the British Library.

ISBN: 9781835694725 (soft cover)
ISBN: 9781835694909 (hard cover)

Printed and bound in China

Discover more at
www.hungrytomato.com

MIX
Paper | Supporting responsible forestry
FSC® C158492

CONTENTS

Chapter 1

ANIMAL DETECTIVES UNITE!

CASE NUMBER #52948
Mystery of the Muddy Mess
CASE STATUS
UNSOLVED
CRIME SCENE

LOCATION:

Riverbank, an area that was once tidy and peaceful.

CRIME SCENE FACTS:

- Detectives were called to the scene of the crime to find tree stumps, trees bent in half, and trees with giant chunks taken out of their trunks. Up close, these damaged trees were covered in flat teeth marks, as if someone – or something – had chewed on the wood to snap the trees like toothpicks. Wood chips were all over the ground but there was no sign of any wood-chipping machinery. Nearby, grass and weeds were crushed and trampled. Narrow channels of mud had been worn straight through the pretty bunches of flowers along the river, as if something had slid down the riverbanks.

- Strangest of all, tree branches with the bark peeled off were strewn higgledy-piggledy and a huge heap of sticks was piled up in the water!

- In the mud at the edge of the water were footprints that looked a bit like hands... but with webbing between each finger.

CLUES:

- Chewed-up trees
- Wood chips
- higgledy-piggledy branches
- Mud slides
- Peeled branches
- Giant heap of sticks
- Webbed footprints

POSSIBLE SUSPECTS:

1. Alien
2. Swamp monster
3. Really angry duck??

What do you make of this cold case? If you don't know much about animals, like the detectives who were first on this scene, you might think this could really be the work of wood-chomping aliens, swamp monsters on a rampage, or a duck with a temper and a weirdly sharp beak!

But that's because this is a job for a detective that actually knows a thing or two about animals.

An animal detective would know that there are very few creatures that could leave behind a scene like the one in cold case file #52948. And they would probably have two things to say:

1. There's only one real suspect, and that suspect is an animal called **a beaver.**
2. There's nothing criminal about this scene: this is just what happens when a beaver does what it does best.

Beavers are just one of many (non-criminal!) animal masterminds we share our world with. They're natural engineers, shaping their environment to suit their lifestyle better. Beavers have a super clever way of making safe homes for their families.

First, they block the flow of a slow-moving river or stream by building a pile of mud and sticks – this is called a dam, and it creates a deeper pool of still water. Then, they build a "beaver lodge" in the pool out of even more sticks and mud. This lodge has a dry area inside and an underwater entrance or two. Pretty snazzy for rodent accommodation!

These lodges protect the beavers from predators – they are surrounded by water and hard to get into, like a muddy fortress! Beavers will even sometimes dig channels in the nearby riverbank for easy access to the best trees to munch on (they like bark, twigs, and leaves).

That way, they can strip and break off pieces of a tasty tree and float them down the channel, straight back to their house. **GENIUS!**

Sounds like a lot of work for fast food… but it's also kind of a brilliant idea.

All of this is even more amazing when you remember that beavers are less than 80 centimeters (31 inches) tall, yet their lodges can be up to 5 meters (16 feet) tall and can house up to 10 beavers!

Beavers can use and add on to dams from generation to generation, or use other beavers' dams that they had nothing to do with building.

And there's a perk for the rest of us, too. The ponds created by the beavers' construction work help control flooding, slow down the wearing-away of rich soil (called soil erosion), and become habitats for other animals like fish, frogs, and birds.

Beavers are awesome, but I can assure you there's no shortage of natural talent like this in the animal kingdom.

LET ME ASK YOU SOME QUESTIONS:

Can you sleep for three whole years to get through a tough time?

Have you ever shouted so loud that you could be heard 5 kilometers (3 miles) away?

Or picked up something, like a car, that weighs many times more than you – then carried it over your head?

Do you change color so that you can blend into the walls or the ground when you're scared?

It would be very surprising if the answer to any of these questions was yes. Unless you're a snail, a lion, an ant, or an octopus, that is! Animal masterminds have some pretty incredible, inspiring abilities that help them survive and thrive in even the toughest situations.

But don't start feeling sorry for yourself because you can only lift a toy car over your head. Humans have their own talents, and one of them is an unmatched ability to learn and invent new things. Which is good news, because animals have a lot to teach us.

We share our planet with millions of other species of animal, many of which scientists haven't even studied yet!

WHAT ARE SPECIES?

A species is often defined as a group of living things that can mate to produce new generations of animals that can also reproduce.

A lion and a giraffe are obviously from different species. So are a chimpanzee and a howler monkey. But sometimes animals are so much alike that scientists need to use DNA – the genetic material in animals' cells that carries instructions for how their bodies grow, function, and reproduce – to decide whether they are members of the same species.

I have weird news for you: humans *are* animals. We share between 50% and 99% of our genetic material, the blueprints for all of our cells, with other mammals.

WHAT ARE MAMMALS?

Mammals are air-breathing, usually four-limbed (but not always), hairy, milk-producing animals with a backbone and a steady body temperature. This group includes humans, chimpanzees, cows, dogs, and even whales... but not fish, birds, lizards, or toads.

It feels sort of embarrassing that we don't have soft fur all over our bodies to keep us warm or long tails to swing from trees with or sharp claws to defend ourselves. We can't even see in the dark or jump very high.

But it's true: we are technically the same kind of mammal as a monkey or a gorilla is – a primate. If we had to compete in the animal Olympics with just our bodies, we'd probably lose most of the events. However, we are the add-on, upgrade experts: our big brains help us solve problems and build tools and devices to give our natural abilities a boost. In this book, when we talk about animals, we're mostly talking about non-human animals. It's just worth remembering that we are technically a part of the big animal party, too!

ANIMAL DIVERSITY

There's an amazing diversity of life here on Earth, meaning there are lots of different kinds of creatures!

There are animals that eat using tentacles, animals that protect themselves with sharp or poisonous quills and spines, ones that can live about 6,100 meters (about 20,000 feet) up a mountainside, and others that can live about 8,000 meters (about 27,000 feet) under the sea.

FRIED-EGG JELLYFISH

It looks pretty much just like a fried egg (no surprise there). But it's a fried egg that can move and eat using tentacles. It just drifts along in the sea looking like breakfast!

PORCUPINE

A porcupine has sharp quills, sometimes over 30,000 of them! These stick up as a warning when the porcupine feels threatened, and come out easily to hook into very regretful predators (animals that hunt it).

LIONFISH

It has poisonous spines full of venom that can sting for days. No one likes this fish, but they're really pretty!

MARIANA SNAILFISH

It lives in a deep-sea trench (the Mariana Trench) where the pressure is 800 times greater than at the surface. This makes it the deepest-dwelling animal.

YELLOW-RUMPED LEAF-EARED MOUSE

It is found at the top of a 6,700-meter (22,000-foot) volcano, making it the highest-dwelling mammal on record. It can keep itself warm without shivering, unlike other mammals (including you!).

KANGAROO

It can leap 9 meters (30 feet) in a single jump and carries its baby in a pouch on its belly.

Somehow, all of these wildly different wild creatures share the same planet!

It's not surprising that there are many scientists that study what animals do. They're a bit like real-life animal detectives, watching animals and collecting clues that tell us more about them. What an animal does is also called its behavior. Animal behaviors that we can study include how they eat, hunt, sleep, play, fight, move around, and raise their young.

Studying these behaviors helps us learn about non-human animals, but it can also help us learn about ourselves.

Like most animals, humans have biological clocks – internal rhythms that (usually) help keep our bodies on schedule to eat, sleep, and feel energetic at the right times of day.

Like many other species of animal, we are social and need interaction with others to stay healthy and feel secure.

Because of similarities like these, discoveries about other animals can inspire research about humans. But we should be careful not to make assumptions.

Assumptions are guesses that aren't backed up with solid evidence. Yes, people are animals. But we can't always say that another animal's behavior tells us about human behavior just because we are also animals, or because we do some of the same things that animals do for the same basic reasons.

Plus, there are more reasons to study animal behavior aside from the fact that it's just super interesting and that it could help us learn about ourselves. Studying animals also helps us understand the world around us better, and shows us how we can change it. Best of all, it can inspire us to protect animals and the future we all share on this planet.

So how do scientists know what to look for when they study an animal? It might be hard to figure this out if you've never studied an animal in detail before.

Let's start completely fresh by taking an imaginary scenario and looking at it in a scientific way...

STUDYING A DRAGON

SCENARIO:

Let's say a dragon has decided to make a nearby park its new home. You might be worried about the trees in the park, first of all, when you see the flash of the dragon's fiery breath in the distance. **But putting that aside, what questions would you need to ask yourself?**

- What sort of things could you learn about dragons if one lived near you?
- No one's ever studied a real-life dragon before, so how would you do it?
- And while you did it, how would you protect yourself from the fire, smoke, and long, sharp teeth the dragon might have, while still gathering useful facts?

APPROACH:

Start by watching from a really dense bush, wearing lots of protective, fireproof gear, taking notes on what the dragon is doing.

FINDINGS:

- The dragon scratched the ground with its claws.
- It cooked a sausage with its breath.
- It built a nest out of (stolen?) picnic blankets.

NOTICING THESE BEHAVIORS WOULD SPARK QUESTIONS, LIKE:

- Why is the dragon building a nest out of picnic blankets?
- How, over many years and many generations, did dragons start to do this?
- What triggered the dragon to build the nest now?
- How did this particular dragon learn to build picnic nests?

Enough, Plonk. It's time for the author to take over again. Dragons may not exist, but these questions are just like the ones animal scientists ask all the time about real animals. And they're the questions that were first asked by some of the earliest modern animal scientists.

Let's take a step back and make a few quick stops on the timeline of studying...

ANIMAL BEHAVIOR

1800s - DISCOVERY

When Charles Darwin, a British naturalist (someone who watches and studies the natural world), joined a five-year sailing trip to explore the coast of South America, he made notes about lots of plants and animals. While the ship was in the Galápagos Islands, Darwin noticed that although similar birds lived on different islands, they had slightly different features that fit the environment of their particular island best. For example, the sizes and shapes of their beaks were suited to the types of seeds found there.

1800s - FINDINGS

This series of observations eventually helped form Darwin's theory of evolution. Darwin found that members of a species with features that fit their environment the best were more likely to survive and have babies. This made sure that those features were passed down to the next generation of animals.

Over many, many generations and hundreds and thousands of years, this led to gradual changes in the whole species of animal. We call these changes adaptations and this process evolution. When animal scientists notice a behavior, they ask why it might have evolved.

1900s - DISCOVERY

At this time, scientists made some really important discoveries by watching animals in controlled environments.

1900s - FINDINGS

Scientists such as Ivan Pavlov discovered that he could train a dog using positive rewards and associations. He would show food to a dog at the same time that he hit a buzzer, causing the dog's mouth to water. Soon, the dog's mouth watered whenever it heard the buzzer, even if food wasn't shown!

PAVLOV'S EXPERIMENT

This taught scientists about conditioning (we'll go into this in more detail later).

MID-1900s - DISCOVERY

Animal behavior began to get more attention as its own area of study, instead of as just a small part of biology. Three of the leaders who drove this change were Austrian Konrad Lorenz, Dutchman Niko Tinbergen, and Austrian Karl von Frisch.

MID-1900s - FINDINGS

LORENZ

Lorenz discovered a behavior called imprinting, which is when birds bond with the first moving thing they see after they hatch. He tested this by leaving half of a clutch of goose eggs under a goose mother and the other half in a warming device called an incubator. When the eggs in the incubator hatched, Lorenz made sure he was the first thing they saw. The goslings followed Lorenz around, even when they were mixed up with the group who saw their mother first instead.

TINBERGEN

Tinbergen made discoveries about bird nesting behavior, but he also came up with a version of the four questions we asked about our dragon earlier in this chapter. He wanted to find out why an animal's behavior was useful to it, how it evolved over time, what things in its environment or inside of its body triggered the behavior, and how it developed or learned it.

VON FRISCH

Von Frisch's most famous work was with bees. He showed that they could tell the difference between different tastes and smells. He also discovered that bees do a kind of dance to show other bees how to get to tasty flower nectar they've found. For a long time, no one knew why bees would do a little "waggle dance" in front of other bees. Von Frisch slowly learned how this dance worked by tracking the journey of individual bees between their hive and food that he left out, and watching the dances that these bees did in front of other bees, who then came to the food themselves.

The bees changed the angles and length of their dances to reflect how far away the food source was and in what direction!

Together, Konrad Lorenz, Niko Tinbergen, and Karl von Frisch won a Nobel Prize for their work in 1973. They're also given credit for being the first modern "ethologists" – scientists that study the behavior of non-human animals, especially in their natural environment.

These days, some scientists question the confidence we can have in these dances, but von Frisch was still a leader in animal behavior. With new evidence, scientists can always build on or challenge the findings of the scientists who came before them.

TODAY - DISCOVERIES

What does animal behavioral research look like today? Well, it can be split into two really big categories: field research and laboratory research.

FIELD RESEARCH

In field research, scientists mostly just watch closely without getting involved. They watch animals in their natural environment to see how they behave.

LABORATORY RESEARCH

In laboratory research, scientists set up experiments to see how animals behave in a controlled environment.

MIXED RESEARCH

Sometimes, research is a bit of both: a scientist might make small changes to an animal's environment in the field to see what happens.

TODAY - FINDINGS

In all cases, scientists today want to see how animals react to different stimuli. Stimuli are signals from an animal's environment or from their own bodies. For example, a loud, sudden noise is a stimulus that might make an animal jump, or run, or prepare to fight.

A pang of hunger is a stimulus that might remind an animal that it needs to find a snack.

Whether they're working in the field or the lab, new technologies are turbocharging the toolkit of animal researchers like never before – more on this later!

Now, let's take a deep dive into

CONDITIONING AND INHERITANCE

WHAT IS CONDITIONING?

You've probably heard of conditioning before, just by a different name. Conditioning is a simple kind of learning where some behaviors are discouraged with punishment or supported with rewards. In this way, the rewarded behaviors become more common.

INHERITANCE

Inheritance, on the other hand, is when living things pass their traits on to their babies naturally, through their DNA. Instead of learning it through conditioning or having it taught to them, animals are simply born with inherited traits and behaviors.

NATURE VS. NURTURE

Some people also call this split nature vs. nurture. "Nature" is an animals' inherited behaviors and "nurture" is the process of teaching and encouraging an animal to behave in certain ways.

Many scientific debates have come from these ideas.

They make us ask questions like:

If an animal had been raised in a different environment, would it still behave this way?

OR

Would a dragon still breathe fire if it grew up in your attic and was taught that it was very rude to burn down a house?

Chapter 2

COOL TECH IN THE FIELD

Cutting-edge technology can make a huge difference when scientists study animals in the wild.

LET'S TRAVEL BACK IN TIME...

JANE GOODALL

Jane Goodall was an animal scientist who was one of the first people to observe chimpanzees in their natural environment, starting in 1960. And she did this for longer than anyone else ever had, spending lots of time earning the trust of the animals and learning new things about them.

One of the most important things that Goodall learned was that chimpanzees can make and use tools. This is something that we didn't know before she watched them doing it.

All of this was no easy feat: At first, the animals were very shy and difficult to find, and Goodall had to be very, very patient and careful. Her long-running chimpanzee study began over 65 years ago. This makes it the longest-running wild primate study, ever!

Here are a few more famous animal scientists that did (or are still doing!) field work:

JEAN HENRI FABRE

Fabre was a French entomologist, which is the kind of scientist that investigates bugs. And yes — bugs DO count as animals, just very creepy-crawly ones! He studied insects to learn about how they communicate and did experiments with them, changing their environment to see what they would do.

EXAMPLE:

He took caterpillars that naturally follow one another and arranged them in one big circle to see how long they might walk that way.

The result: they kept moving until they were no longer able to carry on. It was a harsh experiment, but it revealed just how strong this behavior was.

EUGENIE CLARK

Clark was an American ichthyologist (a scientist who studies fish) who spent much of her career diving with sharks and observing their behavior. She debunked the myth that sharks need to keep swimming in order to breathe and made new discoveries about how they learn. She made 72 submersible dives (a submersible is a small underwater vehicle) and spent lots of time on land too, helping people understand sharks better.

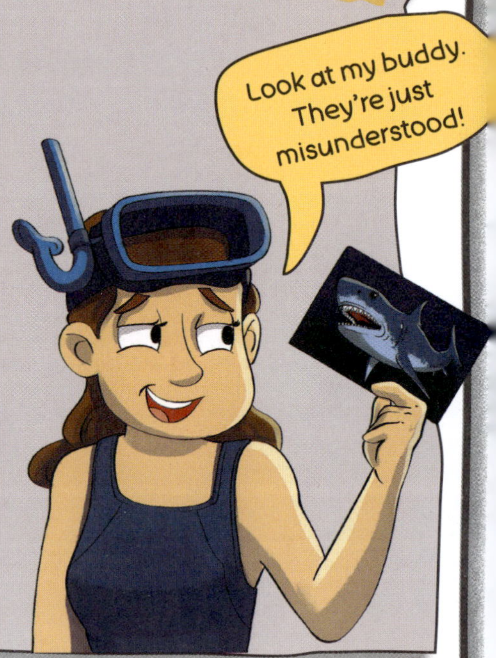

TSUNEMI KUBODERA AND KYOICHI MORI

Kubodera and Mori are two Japanese scientists who managed to get the first-ever photographs of the mysterious giant squid. The squid attacked the bait they'd attached to their cameras, giving them useful information about how the creature hunts and eats, too.

The most important requirements for field research are:

- THE ABILITY TO WATCH VERY CAREFULLLY
- OBSERVATIONAL SKILLS
- GOOD, CLEAR NOTES

Bet you didn't notice that there was an extra letter "L" in the word carefully, did you? You did! Well then, you are on the right track to becoming an animal scientist!

Field researchers should make sure they understand the possible dangers of the field, too, like extreme weather, landscapes, or risks from the animals themselves. Some field studies might involve changing an animal's environment in small ways to see how they will react to the changes, but researchers should always make sure not to endanger the animals or damage the environment through their work.

Where can animal scientists do field research?
Well… just about anywhere they can find animals!

Let's go on a little trip to explore just a few of the biomes (places with similar landscapes, climates, and plants and animals) that animal scientists might study in…

TROPICAL RAINFORESTS

True to their name, tropical rainforests are... wet, and full of trees. They're also hot, and chock-full of plants and animals (more than half of all the species on Earth live in tropical rainforests). Leaves stay on the trees there all year round, which means there are lots of places for animals to hide.

THINGS YOU MAY FIND:

- Trees and plants. Lots and lots of them.
- Animals. Tons of them - possibly including one (very polite-looking) proboscis monkey...

GRASSLANDS

There are a lot of plants and animals in grasslands, too, even though grasslands tend to be much drier. They're even too dry to support many trees, but they're a good place for herds of big animals that eat – you guessed it – grass.

THINGS YOU MAY FIND:

- Grass. Lots and lots of grass.
- Lots of sun - no shade, sorry!
- Animals. Herds of them - possibly including a very hungry, very rude buffalo... talking with its mouth full of grass.

WETLANDS

A wetland is an area that is usually partly or fully covered by water and includes swamps, bogs, marshes, and mangroves. Lots of plants and animals live in them, including many types of birds, reptiles and amphibians, fish, and mammals, like otters, muskrats, and our clever engineers – beavers.

THINGS YOU MAY FIND:

- Water, mud and more water.
- Animals – possibly including a rare sighting of a farting frog... yep. You read that right!

DESERTS

Deserts are always dry and often hot during the day. Not much can grow in a desert, and many animals wait until night time to come out. Animals that can burrow underground during the day and go a long time without water do better in deserts.

THINGS YOU MAY FIND:

- In-your-socks kind of sand.
- Cacti. Spiky, prickly, and not huggable.
- Animals – possibly including one very determined meerkat... still digging the same hole he started last Tuesday.

OCEANS

Also called the marine biome, it's the most common one on Earth because oceans cover most of our planet's surface! It's a biome with many zones because different types of animals live at different depths.

THINGS YOU MAY FIND:

- Water. Deep, blue, and full of mystery (and fish poo).
- Animals. All shapes and splashy sizes – dolphins, jellyfish, whales, and maybe even some toothy sharks.

Field scientists face special challenges. It can be very hard to reach some animals' habitats – the places where they live. For example, some places are very dangerous, like the top of a mountain... or the bottom of an ocean trench.

Some areas are so big that a scientist would have to search for a long time to find the animals they're looking for. A rainforest for example might only be home to a few of the type of animal a scientist is looking for, and that animal might be even harder to find and observe because of thick leaves or steep valleys.

The extreme weather conditions of some habitats might make it hard to use certain devices and technologies. Or they might require extra-special, extra-expensive equipment. For example, some animals live so deep in the ocean that you would need a submersible. All of the water pushing on anything that goes that deep makes it a very dangerous place to visit. Because of this, scientists know very little about deep sea animals. In fact, a study calculated that 99.999% of the deep seafloor has **NEVER** been seen by humans!

Scientists don't get to make many observations of the deepest sea creatures. That alone makes them mysterious. But the images we have of these animals show they're unlike anything closer to the surface. **Take a look at some of these otherworldly (and, let's be honest, a little bit scary) cases...**

SUSPECT NUMBER #34645

THE LURER - ANGLERFISH

STATUS AT LARGE

SUSPECT PROFILE:

- It is named for the bright lure it dangles in front of its face to catch prey.
- An angler is another word for someone who fishes using a fishing pole.

SUSPECT NUMBER #12821

MASTER OF DECEPTION - SEA ANGEL

STATUS **AT LARGE**

SUSPECT PROFILE:

- They look like floating, glowing angels, until...
- They shoot out tentacles and gobble swimming snails!

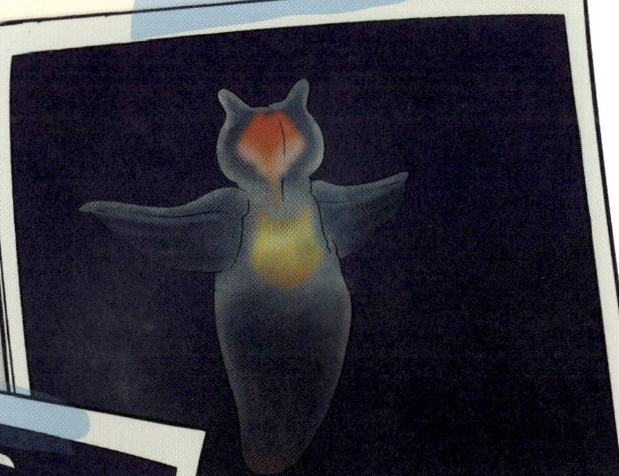

Looks like an angel?

SUSPECT

SUSPECT NUMBER #19980

PREY SLAYER – RED CROWN JELLY

STATUS AT LARGE

CRIME SCENE FACTS:

- It is a jellyfish that flashes blue lights when it gets scared, a behavior scientists think might scare predators away or draw attention to the predators... to turn them into prey for other predators!

The good news is that modern-day scientists aren't on their own when they come up against these challenges: they have lots of cool tech to help them in their investigations. When it comes to deep sea exploration, remotely operated vehicles (meaning there's no human driver inside – humans can drive it from afar) can now shine lasers that analyze the bodies of organisms and their movements.

This means that even though scientists can't physically spend time at those depths themselves, they can reach them virtually. There are now even devices that can catch, sample, and release small deep-sea creatures in their natural environment.

These methods may eventually replace older and riskier practises of bringing animals up to shallower depths or the surface to be studied, which can damage or kill them.

Let's look at an animal scientist's tool kit. What technologies and resources can they use to make their observations and gather data (facts and measurements) in the wild?

FIRST THINGS FIRST: Before they even think about turning on a device, they may want to call on local knowledge. This means that they might get in touch with the community that lives near the animal they want to study. They might ask them if they are willing to keep track of how many of the animals they see and where they see them.

FUN FACT: AMAZON FINDINGS

A recent study in the Amazon rainforest surveyed 19 different villages to see what the people who lived there could tell them about some of the mammals, birds, and reptiles in the area. The local knowledge they gathered helped scientists understand and predict the species' populations.

ANIMAL SCIENTIST TECHNOLOGY:

Scientists studying animals use a wide variety of technologies. Some of these have been around for a long time in some form, like:

CAMERA TRAPS

These are cameras that scientists set up and then leave behind. When something moves or gives off heat, camera traps start recording video or take a picture automatically. This way, they might capture images of animals that are usually really good at hiding!

GPS TRACKING USING SATELLITES

GPS stands for "Global Positioning System". Scientists can attach trackers to animals that send signals to satellites, which are spacecraft that collect information and can pinpoint the location of those signals. These satellites then send information back to researchers about where the animals are and how they're moving around.

PROJECT: EAGLE GPS

A few years ago, Russian scientists using GPS trackers to learn about the migration patterns of eagles ran into an unexpected problem. They had planned to have the trackers use text message data to send information back to them.

FINDINGS

But when the eagles flew out of mobile data network range, they racked up huge data roaming charges. Luckily, the phone company gave the team of volunteer scientists a big discount and saved their research budget.

TRANSMITTERS

Other kinds of electronic devices called transmitters can be attached to animals. They can send information about an animal's location but also sense things about an animal's body, like temperature, heart rate, how fast they run, or how deep they dive. They can send their information to a data receiver using radio waves or satellites.

In this instance, a transmitter would tell you that the racoon was cold, had a fast heartbeat, and was in the wrong environment.

ACOUSTIC SENSORS

These are similar to camera traps, but for sound. They can record animal sounds in remote locations.

NEW TECHNOLOGY:

Some technologies are much newer, including updates and supports for the older technologies:

DRONES

Remember how hard it is for those scientists to trek out into remote locations to find animals? Unmanned drones – meaning they have no human on board – can be flown into remote areas to take different kinds of pictures, capture audio, or even make noise to get a reaction from animals. They are an improvement on camera traps in that they can take in many more camera angles at once. They can also record lots and lots of information quickly. Some drones can also collect samples and measure and tag some animals themselves. Camera traps are still useful in that they can be left somewhere for a long time and don't have as many legal restrictions as drones sometimes do.

FUN FACT: DRONE AUTOMATION

Researchers programmed a drone flying above a conservation park in the United States to independently detect animals based on training data from a research center in Africa. When it located the target species, it was able to follow and keep those animals on camera, without needing remote human help.

PROJECT: WHALE SNOT COLLECTING

Another United States-based project uses drones to collect biological information from whales. The drone flies through the whale's spout, which is the air it breathes out when it comes to the surface.

FINDINGS

As it flies, it captures DNA. It also captures tiny living things that live inside whales. The information scientists get from these samples gives them clues about a whale's health.

ARTIFICIAL INTELLIGENCE (AI)

Artificial intelligence is kind of a fancy term for when computers do things you would only expect people to be able to do, like learn patterns and solve problems.

Artificial intelligence can help scientists look through all of the data from drones and satellites and pick out the things that they should pay special attention to. Tracking animals used to be a very slow process, but one of the things speeding it up is AI.

FUN FACT: AI IN WILDLIFE

Authorities are even using AI in some places, like Malaysia and Zambia, to monitor endangered animals and protected wildlife areas. It helps them to keep track of these animals and to cut down on poaching activity. The computer is taught to recognize animals and signs of illegal activity so that less manual (meaning it's done by a human rather than a computer) monitoring is needed.

IMPLANTABLE ELECTROCHEMICAL MICROSENSORS

WORD BLOCKS:

Implantable – This means that something can be put inside of a body.

Electrochemical – This means that it interacts with the chemistry in a body and finds and sends information about it using electricity.

Micro – This means that it is very small.

Sensor – And this is just a word for something that takes and sends measurements.

Whew. Say this one three times fast. These implants can give scientists important information about the inside of an animal's body. They're pretty easy to implant, not painful, and let scientists monitor animals non-stop instead of just every once in a while. They can collect information about blood sugar levels, how well an animal is breathing, body temperature, and can even pick up signs of infection!

FOOTPRINT RECOGNITION TECHNOLOGY

Scientists can now feed lots and lots of pictures of animal footprints into computer software to teach it how to recognize the tracks of different species. With enough data, the computer software can identify what animal a footprint probably belongs to and keep track of the movements of different animals based on the footprints it spots. This is just one area in which AI can be really helpful, too.

ACOUSTIC SENSOR UPDATES AND RECORDING ANALYSIS TECHNOLOGY

The acoustic sensors we already mentioned have become a lot better recently. The sensors are now smaller and lighter, with a longer battery life. Scientists now also have the technology to filter out background noise and use AI to recognize certain animal calls.

PROJECT: ANIMAL EAVESDROPPING

New computer programs can take lots and lots (and LOTS) of recorded noises and group those noises by type.

FINDINGS

Some scientists hope to use AI to decode the sounds that animals make and translate them into language we can understand. They can then try to link them to certain behaviors or find patterns they have in common with music and human speech! Imagine if you could someday hold up your phone to your cat and translate its meows.

So that's field research. But animal detectives can also carry out their investigations in a laboratory. Animal scientists that do laboratory research have more control than field scientists usually do. In a lab, scientists design an experiment to make sure that they get clear results and can better pinpoint what is making an animal do what it does. If they change just one thing about an animal's environment at a time, it's more likely that the way the animal acts is because of that change.

Let's look at a couple of...

EXPERIMENTAL STUDIES:

EXPERIMENT: BARNES MAZE

Rat mazes are used to test how smart rats are and how well they remember things by watching how they find their way through unfamiliar and familiar spaces. These mazes have gone through loads of versions since the early 1900s.

FINDINGS/PROBLEMS:

Most of the early ones were either: so complicated that training rats to get through them took forever, likely to give confusing results because they involved special rewards or punishments like pain or fear to move the rat through the maze, or simply required lots of set-up and cleaning.

SOLUTION:

In the late 1970s, Carol Barnes invented a simple solution: Using her knowledge of rats' habit of running from the light toward dark spaces to hide in, Barnes put dark holes all around the edge of the maze. She then placed the maze in a brightly lit room. A rat on the maze runs to what look like holes to get away from the light. But only one of them is an actual hole connected to an escape box below: the rest of the holes are phony. Once the rat finds the right hole, the researcher can test how quickly it finds that hole the next time – if it finds it much more quickly, they can assume the rat remembers it.

Different versions of these tests show scientists different things about how rats learn. Researchers have also used the results of injured or sick rats to help inspire research into human memory and aging-related disorders.

EXPERIMENT: CLASSICAL CONDITIONING

A recent study turned up some possible evidence for what a lot of us have been thinking: our dogs understand us! The researchers put some sensors on dogs' heads. These sensors could record brain activity. Then, the researchers had the dogs' owners show the dog some familiar objects, while saying the objects' names. Sometimes, they would have the owners show the dog an object that didn't match the name.

FINDINGS:

Scientists saw a different type of brain activity for the matching objects than for the non-matching ones! This hinted to them that dogs might really know what some words stand for.

Whether they're doing field or laboratory research, animal detectives have their jobs cut out for them. Using their excellent powers of observation, and some helpful technology, they can use the clues they get from animals to try to solve the mysteries of our non-human friends. We may not share a language or even have the same way of sensing the world, but that's why watching animals closely for patterns of reactions is so useful. You'll see in the next chapters that observing animals doesn't just teach us about them: It teaches us about the environment and can inspire our own dreams and designs.

So put on your detective cap and grab your magnifying glass: let's tune into the signals that animals are giving!

Chapter 3

ANIMALS KNOW BEST

Animals are really good at knowing what's going on in the environment around them. Their survival depends on this, so they've adapted instincts that help them react to small changes without even thinking about it. If we look and listen carefully, animals can tell us a lot about our world and the direction it's heading!

One thing animals can tell us about is ecosystem health. An ecosystem is all of the living things in a particular area and how they interact. A healthy ecosystem is one that is balanced, meaning each living thing can play its part in keeping the ecosystem going.

Some plant and animal species are what we call "indicator species". The word "indicate" means "to point out". **So, what does it mean for animals?**

WHAT IS AN INDICATOR SPECIES?

Indicator species point something out to us about the health of their ecosystem. They tend to be very sensitive to changes in their environment, and won't put up with stresses like rising pollution levels or climate change.

Think about it: scientists think evolution sometimes takes millions of years, but humans have only been making their biggest changes to the world for a few hundred years. Environmental changes, like climate change, which is driven by the fossil fuels we burn for energy, are happening more quickly than ever. And many animals simply don't have time to adapt.

When an indicator species suddenly starts disappearing or moving away, this is a **GIANT RED FLAG!**

WHAT ARE ANIMALS TELLING US?

Different types of animals can tell us about different types of stresses on an ecosystem – if we pay close attention! Before we look at some examples, let's define these two words to help us understand things better:

WHAT IS COLD-BLOODED?

If an animal is "cold-blooded", it means that their bodies don't set their own temperature from the inside, like ours do. Instead, their environment heats them up or cools them down.

WHAT IS A VERTEBRATE?

If an animal is a "vertebrate", it means that they have a backbone. An "invertebrate" has no backbone!

AMPHIBIANS

Amphibians are cold-blooded vertebrates, like frogs and salamanders, that live in water and on land (they're good at both). Their smooth skin absorbs things easily and needs to stay moist. Because of this, they are very sensitive to pollution in the air and water. Toxins (poisonous substances) that they absorb can hurt them, so when they start to get ill or decrease in number in a particular area, we can guess that pollution is rising there. Clever!

AQUATIC INVERTEBRATES

Aquatic invertebrates are creatures that live in the water and have no backbone, like water bugs or baby insects that grow up before leaving the water. These guys are tough and many, and you can find lots of them in watery areas... unless those watery areas are polluted!

A really strong indication of water pollution is when we only see the most pollution-tolerant aquatic invertebrates in a body of water... It means everyone else has taken their wiggle party some place cleaner. And if the wiggle party is elsewhere, so are the animals that depend on the wiggle party for food: fish, birds, and maybe some small mammals. As well as the animals that depend on the animals that depend on the wiggle party for food... It's a chain, and it goes all the way to the top!

Hey – bet you didn't know that coral is an animal! Coral is an animal because it cannot make its own food the way that plants do. It's attached to one spot, where it builds a hard shell around itself, but it uses itty-bitty arms to catch tiny creatures to eat. It gets its color from algae that move into its tissues when it's healthy. The algae and the coral work together, because the algae removes some of the coral's waste to make its own food.

CORAL

Coral is a really good indicator species, because when the water gets too polluted or too warm, the coral kicks out all the algae. This causes it to lose its color and look "bleached". The coral is still alive but it isn't healthy, and other species soon leave. The reef goes from being a rich, colorful place full of sources of food and shelter to being an empty, pale landscape. Bleached coral is a **big red flag** that a reef is in danger.

BUTTERFLIES

Poor, beautiful butterflies are sometimes even more delicate than they look! Butterflies are quite picky about the types of plants they use in the early stages of their very short lives. This pickiness means they can be extra sensitive to changes in the environment, like pollution or a loss of plants or temperature changes. Because of their short lives, scientists can easily track changes in their numbers across generations, which helps make them a really important indicator species.

INSECT ADAPTATIONS

Adaptations in insects in general can be observed more quickly and easily than in larger, longer-living animals. Researchers are currently looking at what they think is the adaptation of heat tolerance (tolerance is the ability to put up with something) in fruit flies.

FINDINGS

They're finding that these little creatures are changing at a rapid pace from generation to generation, strengthening traits that make them better at dealing with heat. Studying these adaptations can give scientists ideas in a couple of ways. It shows them how much climate change can stress animal species and how flexible (or inflexible) animal species might be when faced with these changes.

OWLS

Owls are yet another good indicator species. When numbers of some types of owl fall in an area, it can be a clue that the rest of the food chain is in trouble there. Owls (and other birds of prey) usually need plenty of small mammals to eat and good places to build their nests. If the number of owl nests decreases, it's a pretty good bet that the ecosystem is not healthy, either because there isn't enough to eat, or because something is destroying the places they would normally build their nests.

Even the distance between nests can be an indicator of ecosystem health. Where there is lots of prey available, owls can build their nests closer together – basically, there's enough food to go around! But in areas with less food, owls tend to build their nests further apart because they need more territory to themselves. There just isn't enough food to share, and these wise birds can tell!

FUN FACT: CANARY IN A COAL MINE

Have you ever heard the expression "canary in a coal mine" used to talk about an early warning of something? Well, there's a rather sad, interesting, dramatic history behind it. A canary is a little yellow songbird, by the way (shown below).

Let's go back in time to the 1900s. Back then, coal miners would take canaries down into the mines with them. Why? Because miners were always in danger from poisonous gases that they couldn't see or smell, like carbon monoxide. Canaries are more sensitive than humans to these gases, so they would quickly show signs of being poisoned if the gas was present. This gave miners an early warning that they should get out of the mine right away. Without these canary heroes, many more humans would have died in the mines!

Canaries are no longer used in mines, both for ethical reasons and because miners now have access to good, sensitive electronic gas detectors.

Lots of animal scientists have put together projects to study indicator species. These projects are helping them keep track of ecosystem health.

Let's look at a couple of...

INDICATOR SPECIES PROJECTS:

PROJECT: HERRING GULL EGGS

Herring gulls fish from the surface and shores of lakes, and the food they eat has a direct effect on their eggs' quality. For decades, animal researchers collected one egg from each of 14 different groups of herring gulls. They tested the eggs to see how dense they were and how much energy they contained in the form of fats and proteins. Over the years, they saw a decline in the quality of the eggs.

FINDINGS

They were able to link this to a decline in the quality and availability of the fish the birds were eating, which in turn hinted at environmental changes like pollution in the water or a change in the interactions of different types of fish in the lake. For example, larger fish were recently introduced to support sport fishing in the lakes... but these fish eat the little fish that make up a huge part of the herring gulls' diets. Who would've thought these squawky gulls could be so helpful for science?!

Herring gulls are just one example of a species that can show us the domino effect that can happen when ecosystems are thrown out of balance. Another project is a lot… poopier.

PROJECT: PIKAS

A group of researchers in Canada is studying pikas, a rodent that looks a bit like a very small bunny with shorter ears, to learn more about climate change. Pikas thrive in rocky places with little vegetation and plenty of snow. As climate change causes forests to grow at higher altitudes than before, pikas lose their natural habitat and have to move higher and higher up the mountain.

FINDINGS

Pika poo may offer clues to how quickly this is happening! Researchers are developing a tool to detect genetic information in the poo. Genetic information can tell us about the traits that are passed down from generation to generation. For example, your genetic information might tell you that you inherited your weirdly shaped pinkie toe from your grandmother.

Pikas' genetic information can help scientists track an individual animal to see how it's moving around and how tough it is when environmental conditions change.

Observing the way that animals react to environmental change can help us to help them and to make smart choices about healing damaged ecosystems.

PROJECT: ACOUSTIC MONITORING

Scientists are using acoustic monitoring, plus AI, to record marine environments and make decisions about ecosystem health. These projects can capture and tell the difference between noise pollution from boats and equipment and animal noise from whales and dolphins. (Though it might not be able to tell the difference as well if whales decide to start impersonating boats!)

FINDINGS

This helps scientists map the interaction between shipping routes and other human activity on the sea and the activity of marine life. Too much noise pollution can scare or confuse whales, dolphins, and fish, or drown out the noises they make to talk to each other. This may cause them to get lost, have trouble finding one another and finding food, and to leave big areas altogether.

Marine animal sounds can help show us how well an ecosystem is putting up with extra stress caused by human noise and activity. We are a very noisy bunch! Acoustic monitoring can also be used to warn ships as they enter an area full of marine life, so that they can take steps to make less noise or avoid the animals. Some engineers are even hard at work on designing quieter ships. As acoustic monitoring gets even better, it should also tell scientists more and more about marine animal behavior. (And hopefully we won't overhear the animals talking about us too much...)

Animals may be able to warn us of natural disasters that are about to strike. New data is starting to provide evidence for what many people have long suspected or reported: that some animals can sense natural disasters long before humans can!

PROJECT: ICARUS

The ICARUS (International Cooperation for Animal Research Using Space) project is a system of trackers that monitors thousands of animals all the time. It uses solar-powered trackers that send information to and from satellites.

FINDINGS

Data has been found showing farm animals' movements got unusually restless leading up to earthquake and volcano activity. One future aim of the project is to continue tracking these events, and build up an early warning system for humans based on the data patterns.

INCIDENT NUMBER #19980

BATS GONE BATTY

CONCLUSION FASCINATING

INCIDENT REPORT:

- Recently, scientists from the Max Planck Institute of Animal Behavior (managers of the ICARUS project) tracked the spring migration of European bats using lightweight sensors. These bats travel thousands of miles each year and can record temperature as well as location. Pretty impressive for animals whose brains weigh less than a pea, don't you think?

- **The researchers noticed something mysterious in the data:** Some nights showed a huge spike in bat movement, and they didn't know why. When they looked more closely, they noticed that bats were quick to get on the move on warm nights that came before storm activity. Such weather conditions create warm winds that boost the bats' flight so that they don't have to use as much energy. Without the data from the sensors, scientists might have never noticed this trend.

Solving mysteries like this can give us information we can use to protect bats from harm. For example, if they knew that lots of bats were on the move during a particular time period, wind farms could temporarily turn off their turbines to keep bats from getting hit as they pass through!

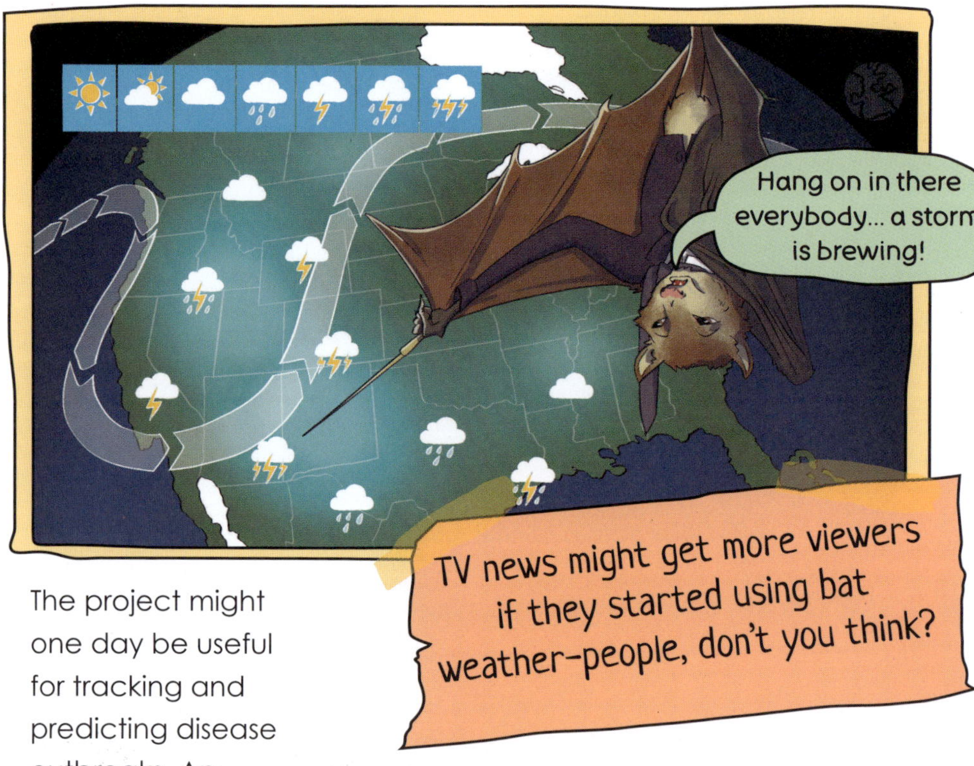

The project might one day be useful for tracking and predicting disease outbreaks. An outbreak is a sudden increase in the number of cases of a disease in a certain area or areas. Wild birds can spread avian flu, so the ability to keep track of their migration patterns would be super important information to have in an outbreak.

The ICARUS team believes they're building an "internet of animals" and that improvements in the information that sensors can capture will continue to make animal research faster and smarter.

ANIMAL TEAM-MATES

Beyond acting as environmental monitors and early-warning messengers, animals can be our team-mates, too. Every once in a while, animals and humans use their natural talents to work directly together.

HONEYGUIDES

Some groups of people in East Africa have a very chirpy team-mate when it comes to harvesting honeycomb. It's a little bird called the honeyguide – a great name, because it does guide people to honey! Honey hunters have learned special calls to get the birds' attention. Scientists have even found that honeyguides will respond better to the specific calls of hunters from their local area. The birds and hunters then work together. The honeyguide leads the hunter to a beehive, where the honey hunter has the tools to get around the bees (often with smoke) and remove the honey from the hive. The hunter gives the bird some beeswax, which it likes to eat, as a reward. This reward keeps it coming back to help when it's called! We'll learn more about working with animal abilities in the next chapter.

DOLPHINS

In some parts of the world, humans and wild dolphins fish together. Here's how it works: dolphins herd the fish from deeper water toward a human waiting with a net in the shallows. As the humans catch the fish in their net, the dolphins pick up the strays that manage to get away!

DOGS

Our friendly relationship with dogs started a long, long time ago, when humans learned to live alongside, and maybe even team up with, wolves! Some scientists believe that a now-extinct type of wolf and humans used to hunt together, with wolves chasing down the prey to tire it out and humans making the final kill. Both species would share the meat. Just like that, a beautiful friendship was born!

Can you imagine if a modern dog were sent back in time to meet early humans...

Knowing how much animals can be affected by human activities also means that we have the ability to protect ecosystems. There are lots of ways to do this, but none of them are easy. We'll need teamwork and commitment to make sure that human activities have less of a negative impact on the environment!

We can make good rules around how to manage waste and how to clear land so that it doesn't pollute or destroy animal habitats. We can develop vehicles that use cleaner energy and make less noise so that we don't drive climate change and disturb animal communication.

We can teach one another about how the members of an ecosystem depend on each other to keep things balanced and healthy, and how we often play an oversized part in this balancing act.

We also need to understand that when ecosystems change, animals may have to adapt **very quickly**. That if they can't, they might not make it! Although animal masterminds are super resourceful (which means they're able to come up with solutions really quickly), they may still need our help to survive. Luckily, we can use what we learn about their instincts and their adaptations to help them to survive!

Chapter 4
INCREDIBLE INSTINCTS

So, what ARE adaptations and instincts? We talked a little bit about adaptations in Chapter 1 when we met Charles Darwin.

WHAT IS ADAPTATION?

An adaptation is a change that happens to an animal over many, many generations to make that animal more successful and more likely to survive in its environment. Changing in this way is also called evolving.

Here are a few examples of some...

INTERESTING ADAPTATIONS

LEAFY SEADRAGON

ADAPTATION:
It has evolved to look like the seaweed it lives in so that predators won't notice it.

REASON:
We can guess that generation after generation, seadragons that looked the leafiest were the least likely to get eaten by confused predators, leading to their current, frilly look.

BLOBFISH

ADAPTATION:

This fish probably evolved its soft, squishy body because of the intense pressure it's under in the deep sea where it lives. Having all of that water above you would compress you (push in on you from all sides to squish you), so it's better to be soft and flexible!

REASON:

When it's in its natural habitat, deep underwater, it looks decidedly less blobby! In its deep-sea habitat, the fish's body is actually much firmer and more compact – it's only when it decompresses on its way to the surface that it becomes limp and blob-like.

MANED WOLF

ADAPTATION:

It has evolved to have very long legs that help it see over and walk through the long grass where it lives more easily.

REASON:

If it didn't have such long legs, it might move too slowly through the grass and take a much longer time to find food.

What other interesting animal characteristics can you think of, and why do you think they might have evolved?

One type of adaptation that can evolve is an **instinct**.

WHAT IS AN INSTINCT?

An instinct is a very strong natural reaction or ability. Animals are born with their instincts. In other words, an instinct can't be learned – these are things that animals do automatically, behaviors that "come naturally" and are inherited (remember our nature vs. chat from Chapter 1).

HERE ARE SOME EXAMPLES:

Fish have an instinct for swimming. They know how to move through the water from birth without being taught.

SPIDERS

Spiders hatch knowing how to build a web – they don't have to watch it happen first or learn the art of spinning silk.

DOGS

Dogs bark when they're excited or worried, but their parents never had to show them how.

PRIMATES

Scientists think that primates might actually be naturally afraid of snakes: they don't need convincing that slithery, scaly things should be left well alone!

CASE NUMBER #56819

THE CASE OF THE BOUNCING GAZELLE

CASE STATUS **UNSOLVED**

CRIME SCENE FACTS:

- This animal has a very interesting, kind of funny-looking instinct. When a predator like a cheetah or hyena appears, they sometimes seem to bounce straight up and down with their legs held out, before running away. **Doesn't this seem like it would be a waste of energy (and time) when a big hunter is hurrying to eat you?**

CRIME SCENE

POSSIBLE EXPLANATIONS

1. To alert their other herd members that a predator is here.
2. To show the predator that they are super strong and fast and not worth chasing.
3. To confuse the predator, especially when more than one gazelle starts leaping.

It looks pretty silly, but it's a behavior that doesn't usually lead to a gazelle being eaten any more quickly than the gazelles that don't bounce, believe it or not. And there must be some pretty good reasons to do it. Scientists think evolution has rewarded this behavior – it helps gazelles survive their environment, where they're often the focus of fast and sneaky predators.

Understanding animal adaptations and instincts can help us better protect them. By protecting animals, we've also protecting the **biodiversity** of our planet.

WHAT IS BIODIVERSITY?

Biodiversity is the variety of life forms in a certain place. Earth's biodiversity is important because each plant or animal species has its part to play in its surrounding ecosystem, to help keep it balanced, healthy, and more resilient to challenges like climate change.

We can use our knowledge about animal behavior to make smarter plans about our own projects and development.

PROBLEM: ELEPHANT AND HUMAN CONFLICT

In parts of Asia and Africa, elephants and humans often come into conflict because they use the same land. Often, the barriers and methods used to keep elephants off farmland are not very well planned! They might block an elephant's well-worn route or provide few alternatives for the elephant to reach the food or water it wants and needs.

WHY IS IT A PROBLEM?

Farms break up the forested areas that elephants live in and separate them from their water sources. Elephants may trample on the farms, eat crops, and sometimes even attack people that they feel threatened by. Sadly, both humans and elephants have died because of these conflicts.

WHAT ARE WE DOING ABOUT IT?

CAREFUL PLANNING:

Scientists are calling for more careful planning, using what we can find out about elephant behavior. By watching elephants to get information about their territoriality (their feelings of ownership over certain land areas) and food and water sources, we can build better barriers and plan the way we use the land better.

KEEPING ELEPHANTS AWAY:

Some scientists have studied the effect of real beehives or even just the sound of beehives, to discourage elephants from entering an area. Not wanting to be stung keeps most elephants at bay!

USING AI:

Other projects are using AI to help monitor and influence elephant behavior. Camera traps can be set up to send their images to a computer running software that uses AI. The AI software can make a guess at whether it's likely that the images show an approaching elephant that triggered the camera. It does this by matching features of the image to patterns it has stored about elephants' shape, size, or movement. If it decides that images contain elephants, it can warn farmers that elephants are on their way. This gives farmers more time to prepare to encourage elephants to move elsewhere. Unlike older methods, these cameras can provide alerts 24 hours a day that are more reliable and immediate.

ELEPHANT APPRECIATION

While we're here, can we just take a moment for elephant appreciation?

They seem to be empathetic, meaning that they have some understanding of the feelings and abilities of others, and will slow down so that an injured member of their herd can keep up!

African elephants are the world's largest land animal, weighing in at about 6,000 kilogram (over 13,000 pounds)!

Their tusks never stop growing!

They create their own sunscreen using mud and sand!

Their trunks have thousands of muscles, are super sensitive, and can be used as a snorkel!

They can stand 3–4 meters (about 13 feet) tall!

In the animal hall of fame, elephants definitely sweep some award categories.

Another large animal that sometimes struggles to coexist with humans is the polar bear.

PROBLEM: POLAR BEAR AND HUMAN CONFLICT

Because of melting sea ice and the rise of human activity, polar bears are coming further inland than they have in the past.

WHY IS IT A PROBLEM?

They can't get to their normal source of food (seals) and are forced to forage or hunt near built-up areas. This puts them in greater contact with humans, which can be dangerous for both species.

WHAT ARE WE DOING ABOUT IT?

Scientists are using new technology to map polar bear dens from above. They are training AI to recognize polar bears and warn humans when one is getting close to a human area. They're also using trackers to learn what makes a polar bear more likely to end up in these risky situations.

Humans and animals have to share the planet, and this isn't always easy. Humans are reducing the amount of space that animals have to themselves. We also have kind of an ugly habit of getting animals into a lot of trouble when we mess up!

Oil spills are very dangerous for all of the wildlife in the area of a spill. It's poisonous for animals to take into their bodies and it can coat their outsides in ways that damage them, too. Just one spill can kill thousands of animals and millions and millions of fish!

PROBLEM: PENGUINS AND OIL SPILLS

Penguins are one type of animal that often gets caught up in oil spills.

WHY IS IT A PROBLEM?

When they're covered in oil, penguins try to preen. Preening is an instinct that birds have to clean their feathers. But as they try to clean oil off of themselves, the penguins swallow the toxic oil and damage their feathers. Swallowing the oil can make them sick or kill them, and when their feathers are damaged, their skin loses protection from the cold environments they live in.

WHAT ARE WE DOING ABOUT IT?

One organization in Australia watched the behavior of a penguin species called the little penguin during oil spills and got a clever idea to help keep them alive when they get coated with oil. A costume change! Knowing that penguins will try to preen, human rescue teams fit them with tiny sweaters so they can't reach their feathers. This gives the rescuers time to clean the penguins, before they have a chance to swallow oil and damage their coats. *And when I say tiny sweaters, I really do mean tiny sweaters...*

Another hazard for marine animals is bottom trawling. Bottom trawling is a fishing method that drags a giant, weighted net along the bottom of the sea. This can cause damage to the natural habitat there and pick up animals that the fisheries don't even want to catch.

One of these animals is a type of sea cucumber called a sea pig (because being called a "cucumber" wasn't funny enough, I guess). This creature crawls along in the mud, eating bits of things that have fallen to the sea floor.

FUN FACT: WEIRD SEA PIGS AND CRABS

One day, a group of scientists using a remotely operated vehicle to study the life around a sunken shipping container noticed something pretty weird about the sea pigs they saw (OK, something even weirder, because these guys do already look pretty weird). Many of them had baby king crabs clinging to them, especially to their undersides where it was harder to see the crabs. The scientists noticed this more in areas with fewer other hiding places.

FINDINGS

Scientists guess that the young crabs, who shed their shells often and are very vulnerable to being eaten, are using the sea pigs for makeshift protection. So far, it doesn't look like the poor sea pig gets anything out of its stow-aways – how rude! But noticing this behavior gives us important information about how the creatures in this ecosystem are connected. And we know now that bottom trawling that hurts sea pigs will probably also hurt baby king crabs.

Staying in the sea, let's take a look at one of our sensitive indicators again, coral. Saving troubled coral reefs is a top priority for many scientists, which has led to a recent breakthrough.

PROBLEM: LARVAL CORAL REEFS

We know that larval coral (baby coral) looks for chemical signals released by more mature coral to know where they should set themselves up to grow. In a sick reef, not enough of these signals are released, so the babies float on by.

WHAT ARE WE DOING ABOUT IT?

This gave scientists the brilliant idea of creating a chemical gel that mimics these signals. It's still a little early to tell how well it will work, but they hope that painting the gel onto a structure the coral can grow on will help it settle down and grow, restoring sick and damaged reefs.

PROBLEM: INSECTS AND LIGHT

Scientists have recently learned something new about insect behavior that might inspire you to turn off more lights at night. Using high-speed cameras to capture images of insects in flight around different light sources, scientists discovered something kind of surprising. Instead of being attracted to the light like scientists thought they were, the insects seemed to go around it in close circles. They think that this is because the insects were actually trying to turn their backs to the light... but kept getting disoriented.

WHY IS IT A PROBLEM?

The researchers think insects do this because the sky used to be much brighter than the ground, even at night. Insects would use this difference in brightness to keep themselves on course. Modern lighting throws this completely out of whack, confusing the insects and trapping them in a circle!

Fireflies and glow-worms have a different problem with all the lights we leave on: they can sometimes mistake them for a potential mate! Which, of course, distracts them from the wooing of actual light-up bugs they could be doing...

WHAT ARE WE DOING ABOUT IT?

Knowing these things about animal behavior, scientists encourage people to reduce the number of lights they keep on at night outside their homes.

Healthy, balanced ecosystems benefit the animals that live in them, but animals' natural abilities and instincts benefit their ecosystems, too! And if we encourage animals to do what they do best naturally, animal masterminds can even help us achieve our own goals.

ANIMAL MASTERMINDS

SUPER SKILLS:

- Filtering pollution out of water.
- Absorbing substances that contain carbon from seawater to make their shells.

Oysters naturally filter pollution out of water by pumping water through their gills, which are lined with tiny hairs called cilia that trap small particles. These are then processed as food or dumped as waste. This filtering cleans the water. Even just one oyster can filter many liters or gallons of water in a single day!

Oysters also naturally absorb substances that contain carbon from seawater to make their shells. When oysters use these carbon-containing substances to make their shells, they're taking the extra carbon out of the sea and air where it can damage the environment.

WHAT IS CARBON?

Carbon is a chemical element that joins up with other elements to form all living things on Earth. Carbon can also bond with oxygen to make carbon dioxide (or CO^2), which is one of the greenhouse gases we know fuels climate change.

FUN FACT: OYSTER CLEAN-UP CREW

There are now projects worldwide to use oysters to clean coastlines. Oysters have experienced habitat loss and damage, plus overfishing, so this attention helps them to recover, too.

CHOOSY BEE

SUPER SKILLS:

- Helping plants create seeds to grow!
- Making incredibly loud buzzing noises in your ears.
- Extreme pickiness!

Bees are important pollinators, meaning that they help plants create seeds by carrying pollen between two plants of the same type. Most flowering plants need pollinators to do this. Otherwise, they won't be able to make the seeds that will grow into new plants. Bee populations are declining, so it is really important that we figure out how to support them better!

Knowing how bees choose flowers to land on can help us make them better pollinators. And it turns out that the bees make lots of silly decisions about which flower to land on, like judging the flowers based on the other flowers surrounding them! Knowing these patterns can help farmers plant their crops in smart ways. For example, they might plant their crops alongside flowers that tend to appeal less to bees, to make the crops seem more appealing.

Another very useful animal instinct is wild horses' and donkeys' habit of digging wells in dry areas to search for the water they need to survive. For a long time, humans treated these wild animals as a nuisance because of the way they trampled the land and took over large areas. But a recent study shows that the wells the wild horses and donkeys dig can increase the amount of water available for all of the animals in the area and encourage new plants to grow. It's not clear whether this ability outweighs the negatives of having those pesky donkeys and horses around, but it's a hoof in the right direction!

SPACE BEAR

SUPER SKILLS:

- Super extreme!
- Old (like your grandparents).
- Living in harsh conditions (including outer space).

Tardigrades, also known as "water bears", are tiny creatures, so small they can just barely be seen by the human eye. They were named for their very slow way of moving – they kind of plod along on their short, stubby legs (an Italian named them "tardigrada", which comes from the Latin for "slow walker"). They live in water or on moist surfaces (for example, in damp moss). But the coolest thing about them is that they are super extreme!

Tardigrades have been around for hundreds of millions of years (not many other animals can say this!) and can be found in the harshest conditions on Earth: in deep ocean trenches, on mountain tops, in extreme heat, in volcanoes, in places high in dangerous radioactivity…

Um, how, you ask?! Well, in extreme conditions, tardigrades can dry out completely, or freeze, or go a long time without any nutrients. Tardigrades can enter a special state where they can basically wait things out until they come alive again in better conditions! This is called cryptobiosis. (Wishing you could just go into cryptobiosis to skip annoying assignments? Me too.) Tardigrades can even survive in outer space, which no other animal we know of can!

WORD BLOCKS:

Crypto – from a very old word meaning "secret or hidden"

Biosis – from a very old word meaning "life mode"

Cryptobiosis – a state in which signs of life are hidden

Scientists have been studying what makes tardigrades so tough in these conditions. If they can learn the answer, it might help us develop stronger crops or better medicine. Tardigrades might hold clues to how we can keep human tissues in good condition leading up to a transplant surgery. They could even teach us how to protect human DNA from radiation, a challenge for some medical treatments and space travel.

Animal masterminds like these tough little critters can give us some pretty amazing ideas. And sometimes, animals simply show us how much better they are at getting some things done!

FUN FACT: ANIMAL MASTERMINDS AT WORK

As we learned way back in Chapter 1, beavers are engineering masterminds. Well, the beavers are back, showing off their talents recently in the Czech Republic (also known as Czechia)! For years, humans there had been making plans to protect a population of endangered river crayfish. They decided to construct barriers that would keep sediment (solid material) and acidic water from spilling into the river habitat from connected ponds. Money had been raised for the project but it was very delayed by paperwork... and then suddenly it was cancelled. Why? Because a group of beavers moved in and built dams that did the exact same job for **FREE**.

Chapter 5
WE'RE THE COPYCATS!

So, we study animals to learn about the world. We study animals to learn about their behavior and to keep them and the ecosystems around them safe. We study animals and… we steal all of their very best ideas. Of course! After all, if an adaptation might be the result of millions and millions of years of evolution, there must be something pretty useful about it, right?

There's a special word for when we copy animals in our designs and inventions.

Copycatting?
No.

Copywolfing?
Very much no.

IT'S CALLED BIOMIMICRY.

WORD BLOCKS:

bio, from a very old word for "life"
+
mimicry, from a very old word for "imitation"
=
biomimicry, an imitation of life

WHAT IS BIOMIMICRY?

Biomimicry is when we ~~totally copy~~ are inspired by plants or animals to solve our challenges.

Can you guess what some of the first animals we imitated were? Think of an ability that no human has (unless you count superheroes, of course).

If you guessed birds, you're right! It seems like humans have always been jealous of birds' ability to fly.

AIRCRAFT DESIGN

In the late 1400s and early 1500s, a very famous inventor and artist named Leonardo da Vinci wrote that he believed that humans could fly... if only they based their designs on birds. He drew hundreds of sketches showing how flight worked, including designs for flying machines. He never got to build one, but if he'd waited around for a few hundred years, he'd have been thrilled to meet...

...the Wright Brothers! Orville and Wilbur Wright flew the very first successful airplane flight in the United States in 1903. It wasn't very long – just about a minute – but they owe their success to our feathered friends. Their design was partly inspired by the way birds use their wings to rise upward and change direction in air currents.

BIRDS AND AIRCRAFT

Birds' wings have a curved shape to them that increases lift (the force that keeps something up in the air) and the ability to turn. The features of different kinds of bird wings have inspired different kinds of aircraft since the Wright brothers' successful flight over a hundred years ago.

LARGE, WIDE WINGS WITH LAYERS OF FEATHERS, LIKE AN EAGLE'S:

These are perfect for catching air currents and gliding without too much turbulence. Big airplanes and gliders take inspiration from this type of wing.

SHORT, POINTY WINGS, LIKE A FALCON'S:

These have adapted for speed and quick turning. Fighter jets are designed in a similar way.

WINGS THAT MOVE QUICKLY, IN A FIGURE-EIGHT SHAPE, LIKE A HUMMINGBIRD'S:

These allow for hovering and backward flight. When it comes to designing improvements for helicopters, scientists sometimes look at hummingbirds for inspiration.

FUN FACT:
Hummingbirds are the only birds that can fly backwards for a significant amount of time!

It should come as no surprise that the designers of unmanned flying aircraft are taking some cues from birds, too. A research team in the United States is working on making drones that could fly much farther without stopping. How can you make a drone that won't run out of power? You take a cue from the albatross – the bird with an amazing wingspan of up to 3.5 meters (11.5 feet) that can glide for hundreds of miles without flapping its wings!

They spend more energy taking off and landing than actually flying, and steer in a way that uses wind drafts to keep themselves going. Scientists hope to create a drone that has fixed wings and is carried along by the wind like this.

Like flight, so many other innovations inspired by animals have changed our lives. Today, we even have the technology to develop animal-inspired innovations that are a part of our own bodies.

DISCOVERY

A United States-based lab is doing research on prosthetic arms (prosthetic means made by humans) inspired by octopuses. Octopuses have the amazing ability to control and move each of their eight arms independently.

FINDINGS

The researchers are hoping that studying the way this ability will help them to develop prosthetic limbs that people can control using their brains! In a way, we're on our way to making ourselves into superhumans: part human, part animal, part technology.

Biomimicry is helping us to make big leaps into the future in areas like sustainability, health and medicine, and other areas of engineering and technology.

FIRST UP, SUSTAINABILITY.

I don't know if you've heard, but Earth is feeling the heat. Human-driven climate change is an urgent crisis that scientists, engineers, and people from all walks of life, all over the world, are rushing to fight.Sustainability can slow down the scary effects of climate change.

WHAT IS SUSTAINABILITY?

A sustainable practice is one that can continue without doing damage to our planet or running out of the materials it needs. Earth is tired! For example, wind and solar power are sustainable forms of energy because they come from sources that don't run out. They also do less damage to the Earth because they are clean forms of energy – they are an alternative to burning fossil fuels to make electricity. And a more practical solution than paying millions of giant hamsters to run on electricity-generating hamster wheels... We can also make things more sustainable by designing them to be more efficient, meaning they are productive but not wasteful.

Animals have given us ways to make our own clean energy even cleaner, and this brings us to an unlikely pair:

HUMPBACK WHALES AND WIND TURBINES!

A wind turbine is a modern windmill that creates electricity using wind power. Humpback whales have given engineers a way to make the blades of a wind turbine move more efficiently.

Um, does a humpback whale look like it could move quickly to you? Believe it or not, it does! A humpback whale can get up enough speed to jump almost completely out of the water, despite its massive size. How? Here's a hint: the answer is going to flip you out!

The humpback whales' flippers are formed in a way that cuts down on drag (the force holding something back as it moves) and boosts lift (the force that pushes things forward). Scientists have figured out that the key to a humpback whale's speed is the little ridges along the edges of its flippers. These little ridges are called tubercles. Engineers added similar bumps into test designs for a new type of wind turbine blade and found that what worked in the water also worked in the air: the new blades lowered drag by about 30% and raised lift by 8%.

Whales and birds aren't the only animals helping us learn how to move faster through air and water. NASA has taken inspiration from an unexpected source: shark skin! Sharks are covered in tiny structures called dermal dentricles – think of them like little teeth or bristles – that cut down on drag and stop things like algae from clinging to them.

SHARKS AND REDUCING DRAG

Scientists designed a material that mimics shark skin, and it works incredibly well. It helps boats, aircraft, and even competitive swimmers move more smoothly and efficiently. Less drag means less energy is needed to move – and that means less fuel is used, too. A pretty clever solution from one of the top predators in the sea!

Animals have had to find clever ways to survive in harsh environments with limited resources, so we can learn a lot from their awesome adaptations when it comes to designing our own sustainable technology. For example, scientists are taking inspiration from fireflies' light-up bottoms!

FIREFLIES AND LED LIGHT

Fireflies' bodies produce light in a way that is more efficient than many light bulbs. When scientists added similarly-designed elements to LED lights, it made them brighter... without using lots of extra energy.

The fashion industry is one of the world's most unsustainable industries, wasting resources and burning carbon every step of the way. But one very slimy animal mastermind has given scientists a wildly sustainable idea for fashion.

SQUID AND FASHION

A US-based team has discovered a protein in squid teeth (those suction cup thingies on their tentacles) that could make clothing fibers stronger. They might be able to make an artificial version of the protein in the lab... but the squid had it first!

Biomimicry is also helping us solve problems in health and medicine. And the animal world is absolutely chock-full of masterminds in this area of research.

LET'S TAKE A LOOK AT HEALING:

PROBLEM

For most animals, including humans, healing from a major injury can be a tough, slow process. With the help of stitches, our bodies do have an amazing ability to grow even major wounds back together, often leaving only scar tissue and bad memories. Even losing fingers, toes, arms, or legs isn't a death sentence if we can get help fast enough. Doctors know how to reattach fingers and toes in the right conditions, and even an arm or leg can be reattached if everything goes just right (after the accident, that is).

But once a limb or a digit (another word for a finger or toe) is gone, it's gone for good. It's a good thing prosthetic limbs are getting better and better, because human arms and legs can't grow back.

SOLUTION

You know whose arms and legs (and tail, and digits) DO grow back? A salamander's! It doesn't matter how much of its limb comes off, a salamander has the amazing ability to grow it back, like new, instead of scarring over the way human wounds do. Some salamanders can even grow back parts of their heart, eyes, and spinal cord. Although scientists see no way that humans could ever completely regrow a limb, a spine, or an organ on their own, they are studying salamanders' talent for regeneration to help human patients heal large wounds.

PROJECT: AXOLOTL

One of the salamanders being studied for its regenerative abilities is the axolotl, a species native to Mexico and named after the Aztec god of fire and lightning. Legend has it the god disguised himself as a salamander to avoid being sacrificed.

Are they silly-looking? Are they beautiful? Both? You decide.

FINDINGS

The axolotl not only regenerates lost limbs and parts of lost organs, it also never leaves its youthful stage like other salamanders do. You can tell by its feathery gills and webbed feet, which are signs of youth. The focus on these creatures led to their entire genome (all of their genetic information) being mapped recently. Mapping their genome can help scientists find the genes that give them their amazing abilities.

Next up in medicine, everybody's favorite medical devices... needles! (Eek!)

PROJECT: PAINLESS NEEDLES

Researchers in Japan have recently developed a needle that is less painful for injections. It may not sound that way, given it has three sharp prongs with serrated edges, and vibrates as it goes in – but actually this is supposed to be exactly what makes it less painful. The top of the needle, the bit that makes contact with the skin, is actually smaller than in a regular needle.

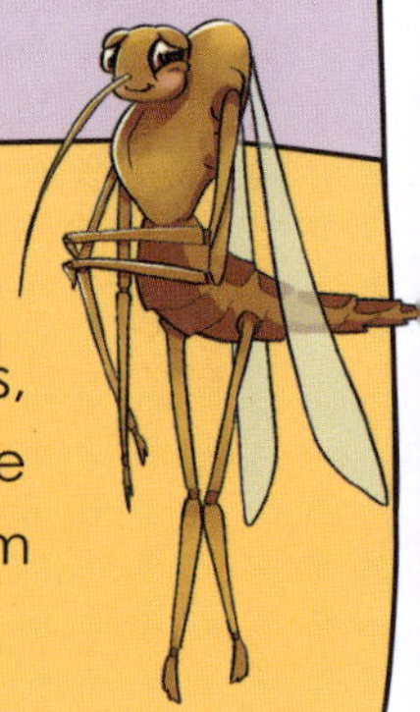

DISCOVERY

How did they come up with this? By watching mosquitoes, everyone's favorite animal! (Yuck!) The design imitates the shape of the mosquito's mouth parts and how it uses them to get to your blood without you noticing.

From a very, very small animal mastermind, we move on to a very big one! Giraffes are next...

PROJECT: GIRAFFE SKIN

Think about how much time and force must be required to move blood all around giraffes' big, tall bodies. They stand up almost all day, too. This puts A LOT of pressure on their feet and legs. But their legs and feet don't swell the way that the legs and feet of humans sometimes do. How!? Well, their skin is very rigid – it's tough and it doesn't move easily – unlike our skin, which is quite soft and flexible.

FINDINGS

Inspired by the giraffe, some scientists created a new, multi-layer compression system for people using elastic wraps. Compression means putting pressure on something, squeezing it. This process keeps blood moving. Someone wearing the wrap should experience less swelling, thanks to the strong skin of the giraffe.

The spider is not to be outdone by the giraffe's strength...

PROJECT: SPIDER SILK

Spider silk is one of the strongest materials… anywhere! It's actually five times stronger than steel, if you compare the materials pound for pound. So, there's very little hope of breaking free if you're an unsuspecting fly stumbling into a spider's web.

FINDINGS

Inspired by the mighty spider, a team of Chinese scientists has recently figured out a way to make artificial spider silk. They've created a protein solution that is as similar as possible to spider silk, with some modifications that keep it from sticking together as much. They use a 3D printer to squirt the solution through hollow needles, weaving the strands together to make an even stronger material… kind of like a big, mechanical spider would! They're hoping to use the material for medical bandages.

Terrible news for arachnophobes (people who are afraid of spiders): spider silk is even used in the military. Because of its strength, various projects over the years have even aimed at making body armor inspired by it!

Spider webs have also inspired another new technology, but this time in service of saving another species of animal. Every year, millions of birds die from flying into glass – they see the reflection of the trees in windows and simply don't realize that they're looking at a solid barrier until it's too late. Poor birdies.

PROJECT: ULTRAVIOLET SPIDER WEB

One company was recently inspired by the way spider webs reflect ultraviolet light (a kind of light that comes from the sun but which humans can't see). This quality is useful to both spiders and birds, because birds can see UV light (their eyes have a special kind of cell in them that ours don't) and therefore steer around spider webs. This means the spider web doesn't get broken by flying birds and the bird doesn't get sticky spider web on its feathers.

FINDINGS

The company has made UV-reflective glass to try to mimic this natural feature. What clever creatures, and what clever humans!

FUN FACT: SPIDER INSPIRATION

Have you ever heard of the tarantella? No, not the tarantula, but you're in the right neighborhood. This is a very strange story. First, you should know that in southern Italy in the 1400s through to the 1600s, a bizarre illness spread. People who'd been bitten by the tarantula spider (technically not the same type of spider that is called a tarantula today) were advised to dance wildly to save themselves from the numbing poison. The weird part? Tarantulas (of past and present) aren't even poisonous. The dance was named the tarantella. If spiders only knew...

But what ELSE, you ask? What, not impressed enough by these animal masterminds' accomplishments in green and medical technology?

Well, we've heard a bit about flying robots imitating birds, but earthbound robots won't be left out of the biomimicry party. Scientists and engineers are drawing on nature for solutions to give them the ability to perform more and more tasks. For example, researchers are working on a common problem for autonomous robots. (Autonomous means that a robot can do tasks without needing a human's help.)

PROBLEM

Autonomous robots have trouble focusing on things set against busy backgrounds or in changing lighting conditions. This is one of the things that makes it hard for them to work independently.

WHAT ARE WE DOING ABOUT IT?

Cats definitely do not have the problem that robots do: they can see well in all kinds of light and are extremely good at focusing on objects. Why? Well, their pupils – the dark part of the eye that lets light in – are narrow slits during the day when the light is bright. This helps them to focus and avoid squinting. At night, their pupils expand to let lots of light in, and they even have an extra special reflective layer on their eyes to boost their night vision.

A Korean team of scientists created a system for robots inspired by these features of cat vision. The result: They found that it reduced the amount of energy the robot needed to process imagery, and that it was better at doing so!

Don't tell the cats you know though – their egos are already big enough.

And cats' eyes aren't the only ones inspiring scientists and engineers, either. A new type of telescope has been developed that takes inspiration from the eyes of a lobster!

DISCOVERY: LOBSTER VISION

Lobsters' eyes have evolved to help them move around and find food in dark, deep, murky water – they're made up of thousands of square, reflective tubes across two rounded lenses. All these cells capture light and focus it onto special structures called photoreceptors. Lobsters' ability to see "well" doesn't really match our expectations – they don't see images so much as movement. But they can capture information from all angles around themselves.

FINDINGS

Scientists hoping to learn about x-rays in space developed instruments based on lobster eyes that can capture a wider view of the sky all at once. They're putting them on satellites to send fast and detailed information back down to Earth.

Lobsters aren't known for their speed, but plenty of other animals are quick and agile. Many of them are also usually either chasing something or being chased, so they need to move around pretty quietly, too. These characteristics came in handy when Japanese engineers looked to the natural world to solve a problem with their high-speed trains. These trains are famously fast: that wasn't the problem...

PROBLEM

The problem was that the trains were LOUD.

WHY IS IT A PROBLEM?

They were so loud and so fast that when they went through tunnels, they would cause a shock wave so powerful that it would damage some tunnels (and the neighbors probably weren't too thrilled, either).

WHAT ARE WE DOING ABOUT IT?

One day, engineers noticed that the kingfisher bird could dive quickly into water to catch fish, hardly making a splash at all when it did. They realized that the bird's long, smooth, narrow beak was letting it slip into the water. They re-designed the front of their trains to look more like a kingfisher's beak.

Eur-beaka! (Sorry.)

The new design was a success – the trains moved faster, quieter, and even used less energy. It made them 20% more energy efficient, and probably made the people living nearby at least 20% more relaxed.

Humans can even take inspiration from their own adaptations. Remember that we're animals, too. You may be a bit sick of hearing about AI, but did you know that the networks of nerve cells that send messages and store memories in our own minds are a huge source of inspiration for building the artificial networks that most AI software relies on? Who's special now, AI?

PROPOSAL NUMBER #409

BULLY REPELLER

PROPOSAL STATUS **REJECTED**

PROPOSAL:

- The horned lizard can shoot blood (infused with the toxic venom of the ants it eats – yikes) from its eyes to scare predators away! We propose to incorporate this into a line of self-protection gear for the school corridor. Bullies, beware! What could possibly go wrong?

THE BULLY REPELLER IN ACTION

Chapter 6

MYSTERIES OF THE WILD

By now animal scientists know A LOT about animals… but they don't know everything. We've already seen that animals can be pretty mysterious. They can be hard to find, hard to watch, and they can't tell us why they're doing something. Even the best animal detectives get super stumped by mysteries of animal behavior. And even the best animal detectives get it wrong!

MYSTERY #9400

WHY DO RACCOONS "WASH" THEIR FOOD?

CASE STATUS SOLVED?

SUSPECT INFORMATION:

Racoons: the mischief-makers of the animal world. They even look a bit like they're wearing a dark mask to hide their faces as they go about causing trouble! Common throughout North America and parts of Europe, they have a reputation for leaving a mess behind them wherever they go.

THE MYSTERY:

Raccoons have an unusual habit. If they're near water when they eat, they will use their very nimble paws (that look a bit like hands!) to dip the food in the water and roll it around a little bit. It looks very much like they're washing their food.

THE INVESTIGATION:

Scientists challenged the idea that raccoons are washing their food by pointing out that they don't always get all the yuckiest stuff off and that they still make the same gesture when they aren't near water. Some guessed that raccoons are instead trying to add moisture to the food to make it easier to swallow, since they don't have glands that make spit the way we do. But then instead, they found something completely different...

THE ANSWER (PROBABLY):

A study found that wetting the skin of their paws, which have loads of nerve endings, actually gave raccoons the ability to feel the shape, texture, and temperature of their food better. Their vision isn't very good, so wetting the food allows them to have a fuller experience of their meal. It also helps keep them safe – these little bandits will eat almost anything, so it's useful for them to have more information about whether something they eat could make them sick!

MYSTERY #52867

WHY DO SOME ANIMALS EAT POO (YUCK!)?

CASE STATUS SOLVED?

SUSPECT INFORMATION:

Speaking of sick... If you have a dog, you might have had an unpleasant experience while walking them. You're strolling along, enjoying the fresh air, when you notice that Fluffy is eating something on the groun — NOOOOOOOOOOOOOOOOOOOOOO!!!

THE MYSTERY:

You can't banish Fluffy. Fluffy is your little poo-eating monster. But you might ask: What the poo is going on, Fluffy!? Don't worry (too much), Fluffy isn't alone — more than 150 other species have also been found to eat poo. This seems... extremely germy and unpleasant, to say the least, right? So why do animals do it?

THE INVESTIGATION:

Well... analysis of poo finds that it's full of water, undigested food (which still contains nutrients), and microbes that can help boost gut health. Microbes (tiny organisms like bacteria) that live in animals' guts help them digest certain foods, especially ones from new environments. This includes humans, by the way, but please don't start eating poo!

THE ANSWER (PROBABLY):

The answer is actually pretty simple, even if the habit feels baffling. Eating poo is a survival instinct: it gives animals extra calories, extra nutrients, and extra microbes that help them adapt to different environments. It's important to notice when Fluffy does this, though. Eating poo could mean that your pet is dehydrated or isn't getting enough nutrients in the diet you're already feeding them!

MYSTERY #23864

WHY DO ZEBRAS HAVE STRIPES?

CASE STATUS **SOLVED?**

SUSPECT INFORMATION:

Zebras are the only striped equids – a group of animals that includes donkeys and horses.

THE MYSTERY:

Scientists just haven't been sure why zebras would have evolved to look the way they do. It's a puzzle that has stumped them for decades, and produced LOTS of different guesses, including that stripes help zebras tell each other apart, that the difference between the temperature of the black and white fur creates air currents that helps keep zebras cool, or that it helps them camouflage themselves.

TESTING A THEORY:

THE INVESTIGATION:

When scientists thought about and tested some of these theories, they were pretty easy to cross off the list. Horses don't seem to have any trouble telling each other apart, so why would zebras need stripes to do it? Scientists find no evidence of air currents across zebra fur, and therefore no cooling effect to explain the stripes. And as they learned more about zebra predators like lions, scientists understood that they probably just see the zebras as a gray outline until they get close enough to hear and smell them, just like they would other prey.

THE ANSWER (PROBABLY):

It turns out that the stripes are great at discouraging a different, less intense-looking threat. Flies! Flies are a nuisance and a danger to equids. They itch and sting and carry disease. From past research, scientists already know that flies don't tend to like landing on striped surfaces. But scientists recently made two key discoveries about zebras in particular. One study showed that zebras living in areas with more horseflies evolved to have more noticeable stripes. And a more recent study found that fewer horseflies landed on zebras and horses wearing zebra-striped blankets than on horses without the blankets. Some scientists feel that this closes the case... but there are also those who still disagree.

Hold on... once a scientist finds an answer to their question or a result to their experiment, isn't that the end of the road? The scientific dream!? Well... not always! Scientists have to stay open to the possibility that their guesses could prove wrong with testing, or that another scientist might gather new information that calls the results that they found into question.

For every solved mystery, there's an unsolved mystery driving animal scientists wild:

CASE INFORMATION

- Did you know that the oldest Gálapagos tortoise on record lived to 177 years old? Tortoises age very slowly and live a very long time, but there are a few animals that can live even longer!
- Meanwhile, the oldest age a human has ever reached is a measly 122 years (and the world-wide average is only about 73).
- Still, that's many times the amount of time that a mayfly can hope to have. Their lives are usually just hours long.

THE ANSWER (YET TO BE DETERMINED):

So why do some animals live for so much longer than others?

Scientists have collected a number of reasons that could lead to a longer life.

- A really obvious one is whether there are predators around to eat the animal (a pretty easy way to die quickly)
- The temperature of an animal's body and living environment (lower temperatures are linked to longer lives)
- Body size (in general, bigger animals live longer)
- Special longevity (the ability to live a long time) genes

But no matter what, here's the truth: scientists are still learning about what the aging process even is. They don't fully understand the biological causes of aging and they can't even agree on whether or not to call aging a "disease".

OLD AGE IS RELATIVE...

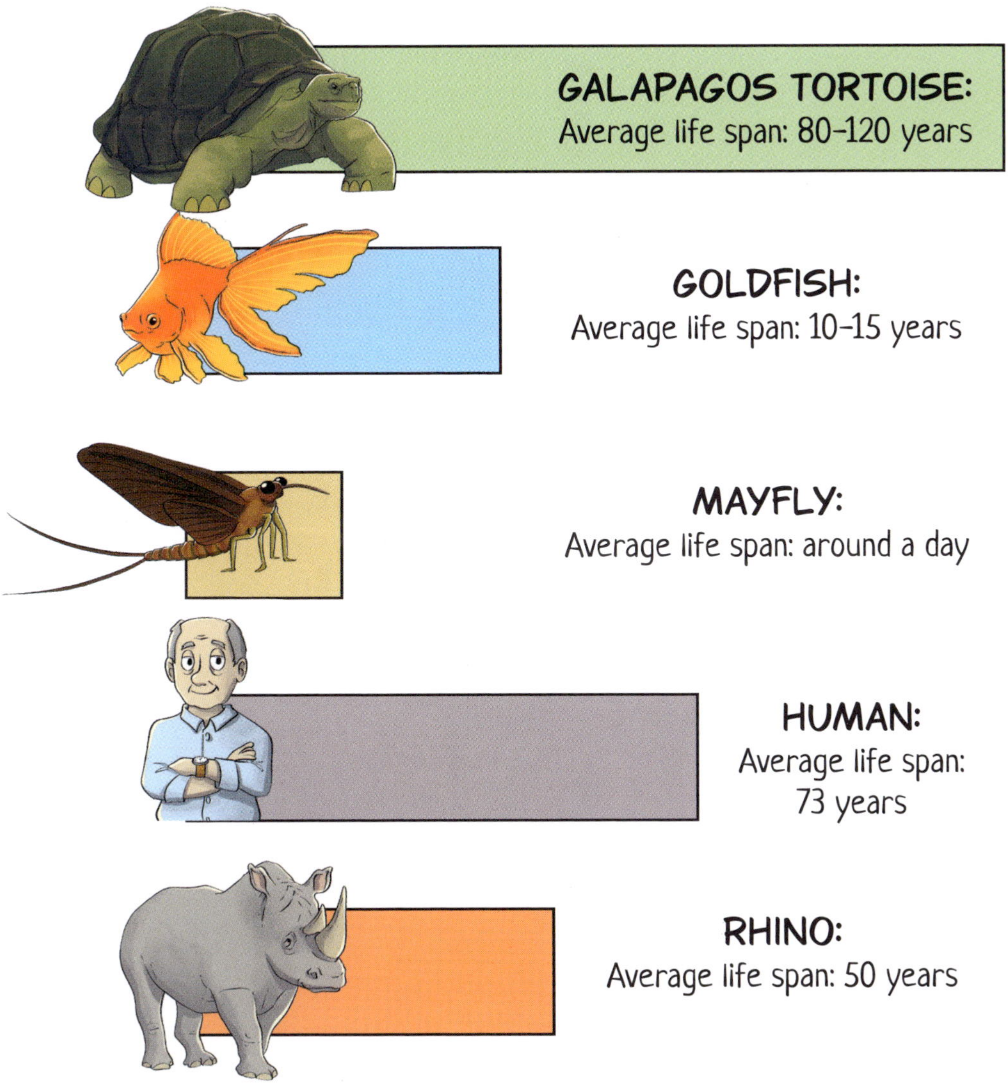

How do you lose an entire species? There are some animals that are either reeeeeeally good at hiding, or have very quietly gone extinct. A species can be considered "lost" if it has not been documented by scientists for 10 years and it isn't in any zoos. There are hundreds and hundreds of lost species, with the list growing longer every day.

MYSTERY #00001

LOST OR MISSING?

CASE STATUS MISSING

THE KOKAKO

Last heard: singing in the New Zealand forests...

THE ICE STAR

Last seen: deep in the Antarctic ocean...

THE LAST DONUT

Last seen: moments before Miguel was caught with icing on his face!

There's hope, though: not all of these species stay lost! These mysteries can be solved. Just a couple of years ago, in 2023, a sniffer dog named Jessie found the De Winton's Golden Mole burrowing on a beach in South Africa. Jessie found the mole with the help of a team of scientists using an environmental DNA (eDNA) technique. Every time Jessie the dog stopped to show scientists that she smelled something mole-like, the scientists would test for mole DNA that it left behind while moving through the sand. Eventually, they tracked the little critter down.

They've since found more of the moles and think the area in South Africa could actually have a large population of them. But the fact that the mole was lost so long makes these scientists feel eager to make sure they're safe. The local area is used for mining, so conservation efforts could be the mole's best chance for a secure future.

You may have seen some headlines about orcas sinking ships. For the last few years, groups of orcas have rammed boats and sometimes sunk them, and no one really knows why. It started with one group of orcas and then seems to have spread, and usually follows the same pattern: a group of orcas approaches a boat, usually a sailing boat or yacht, and rams its rudder until it breaks off. Breaking off the rudder of a boat, though, sometimes puts a giant hole in the boat. Boats don't do super well if they have a giant hole in them, so some of these boats have filled with water and sunk.

As scary as it might be to have big porpoises with sharp teeth attacking (and sinking!) your boat, scientists don't believe that the orcas are trying to sink the boats.

MYSTERY #9478

SUNKEN SAIL BOAT WITH A GIANT HOLE?

CASE STATUS **SOLVED?**

LOCATION:

Under the ocean.

CRIME SCENE FACTS:

Detectives were called to the scene of the crime to find a sail boat at the bottom of the ocean. There was a giant hole in the side of the boat, and the rudder was broken off.

REASON?
They have two main guesses about what's going on here:

1) The original group of orcas who started this behavior had a bad experience with a boat and figured out a way to stop other, similar boats, or

2) They tried ramming a boat and found out that it was kind of fun. In the last couple of years, there have been fewer attacks, so seafarers are hoping it was just a hot whale trend!

CAN WE BRING ANIMALS BACK FROM EXTINCTION USING SCIENCE? You may have seen a famous movie franchise about bringing dinosaurs back from extinction using their DNA. But could something like that really happen? Could extinct animals be brought back to life using science? Well, spoiler alert: we can't bring back the dinosaurs. To de-extinct a species, you need a source of DNA that hasn't broken down. So far, the oldest intact (not broken-down) DNA is 700,000 years old… Dinosaurs went extinct 65 million years ago, so it's not even a close miss.

But scientists have attempted to bring back an animal that went extinct much more recently than the dinosaurs. It's called Pyrannean ibex and it's a type of goat. In 2003, scientists managed to use the last living Pyrannean ibex's DNA to create a clone. Unfortunately, the goat died soon after birth, making this the first animal to go extinct twice.

Some scientists are using gene editing technology to try to bring other animals back in the form of hybrids.

WHAT IS A HYBRID?

When genetic information is missing, it may be possible to combine, or splice, the genes from the extinct animal with a similar animal that is alive today. Splicing the two together makes it a combination of two different sets of genetic information, or a hybrid.

PROJECT: HYBRIDS

One team has been working on splicing genetic material from the long-extinct wooly mammoth into the genome of a modern-day elephant. They even recently announced that they had successfully done this with the even-longer-extinct dire wolf.

PROBLEM

However, other scientists claim that this is actually a bit of an untruthful publicity stunt. They say that the very hybrid nature of these wolves disqualifies them, that it means that they certainly aren't the same as real dire wolves brought back from extinction.

But maybe the bigger debate when it comes to clones isn't whether we can bring extinct animals back to life. It's whether we should. On the one ~~paw~~ hand, it's an awfully big decision for humans to make – what gives us the right to make it? What if the animals suffer? On the other, extinct animals could restore some lost biodiversity to our planet. And some people feel that because humans are the cause of many of these extinctions, they should be the ones to reverse them.

There's a secret, third option: some scientists believe that using DNA to help keep animals from going extinct is a better use of these technologies. By this, they mean that they could use the DNA of threatened animal species that can no longer reproduce to clone more members and keep those species from going completely extinct. What do you think?

ANIMAL MYTHS

Sharing a world with animals means that we all have stories about animals. Stories of our own, or stories that have been told to us. These are not always the most scientific stories (see also: tarantella as a cure for non-existent spider poison). But it's amazing how much staying power myths about animals can have. Let's bust a few:

MYTH: BIRD PARENTS WILL ABANDON THEIR BABIES IF HUMANS TOUCH THEM.

No this is not true. It's still good to leave baby birds well enough alone when they are learning to fly, but birds' sense of smell generally isn't good enough to even know a human has touched its baby.

MYTH: TOADS WILL GIVE YOU WARTS.

No! Warts are caused by a human virus. But some toads do have poison on their skin that can irritate our skin. So again, the tip here is to leave animals alone anyway!

MYTH: WOLVES HOWL AT THE MOON.

Wolves just move around a lot at night, and they throw their heads back because it makes the sound travel further, reaching other wolves miles away.

MYTH: CAMELS STORE WATER IN THEIR HUMPS.

Camels' humps are made of fat, which gives them energy for long journeys. They are still great at conserving water, it's just not stored in their hump like a water tank.

MYTH: THE COLOR RED MAKES BULLS REALLY, REALLY MAD.

This is a rumor started in Spanish bullfighting, where a matador waves a red flag at a bull to make it charge. Bulls aren't made grumpy by any particular color – they're color-blind. You'd be grumpy too if someone made you fight for your life, but bulls are actually just triggered to charge by the movement of the flag.

How would you go about solving unsolved animal mysteries? Maybe one day your own animal detective work will find an answer to one of these cases...

Chapter 7

STUDYING ANIMALS AT HOME

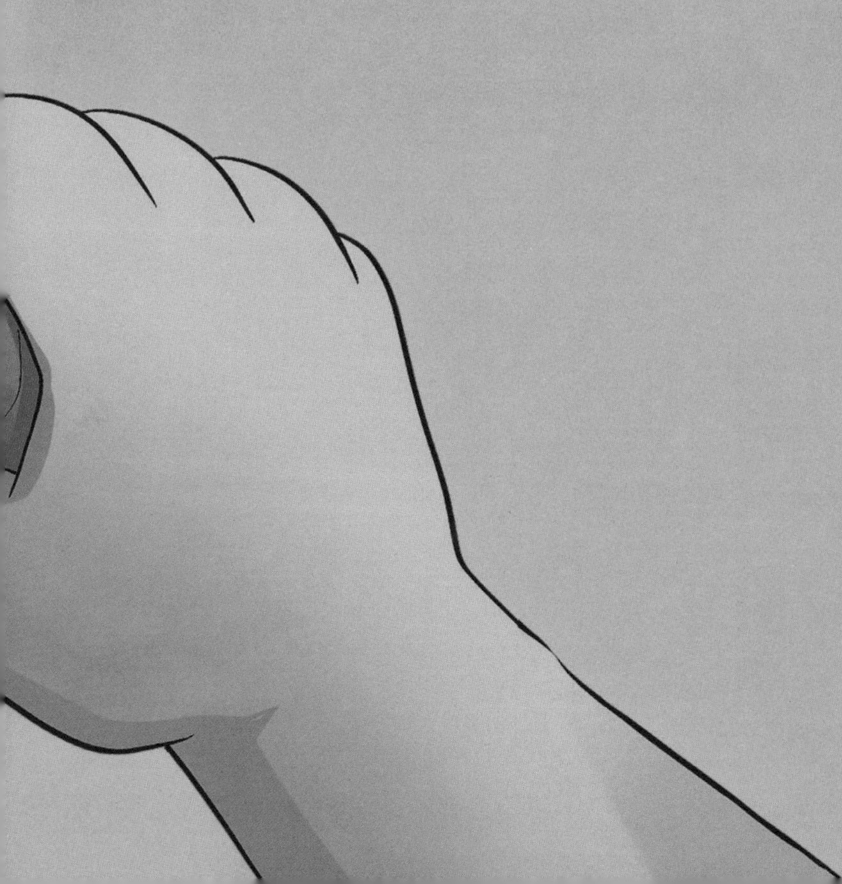

For now, you can kickstart your career as an animal detective at home. You never know, maybe a lost species isn't lost, it's just hiding in your garden! You may not even have to go outside to find animals to study – just think of how many spiders and beetles and ants there could be in your house or room. (If you're not a bug enthusiast, maybe don't think too hard about that...)

HOW TO GIVE BEING AN ANIMAL SCIENTIST A TRY

(in your own backyard or local area, or room)

FIRST, COLLECT SOME FIELD KIT ESSENTIALS.

- Grab a **backpack** or another bag you can zip up and carry easily with you. All the better if it's at least a little bit waterproof – you never know when you might get caught in the rain! Fill it with your essential field scientist tools:

- **A notebook or phone**, for writing down your observations
- **A camera or phone**, for taking pictures (if you don't have either one, try drawing the animals you see!)
- **Binoculars**, for seeing further away – which might be the best way to spot shy animals, especially different types of birds or quiet, nervous animals like deer
- **Water and a snack**, in case you have to sit still for a long time
- **Tape measure**, in case you want to measure and write down how big something is, like a footprint
- **An extra layer of clothing**, just in case you get cold
- **A map**, so you can mark the places that you saw different things

DISCLAIMER

Always be sure to bring a friend with you or tell someone where you're going: even professional scientists do this so that if they end up running from a dragon or falling down a hole, someone will notice they're gone! (The chances of having to run from a dragon or falling down a hole are very low – but never zero...)

Take notes on the animals you see, and ask good questions that you can try to answer by observing the animals. Write down what they look like, what they do, and why you think they look like that, why they do what they do. How do they move? How do they react to other animals, to each other, to different features of the landscape? How do they act in different kinds of weather, and at different times of the day or year? How could you use the technology available to you to measure, track, or expand your understanding of these animals and their ecosystem?

WHILE YOU OBSERVE, MAKE SURE TO KEEP THESE THREE THINGS IN MIND:

1. Animals need many of the natural things in their environment for food and shelter, so be very careful not to disturb or damage anything.

2. Although it might be tempting to try leaving human food out for animals, it's better not to. Wild animals haven't evolved to digest much of what we eat.

3. Don't pick up or touch wild animals, and don't get too close, for your safety and theirs! Even if you see an animal that looks injured, make sure you move calmly and slowly away, then call the authorities.

HERE ARE SOME TIPS FOR FINDING AND STUDYING DIFFERENT TYPES OF ANIMALS.

TOP TIP 1:

Do some research on what animals live in your area, when they are active during the day or year, and what they eat. Look up what their tracks and droppings look like so you can tell whether they've been there recently. For example, spring and fall are a good time to see birds migrating, and snakes shed their skin, usually leaving it behind every few months (or every few weeks if they're quite young).

TOP TIP 2:

See if an adult will get up early with you or stay out as it starts to get dark. A lot of animals are most active at these times.

TOP TIP 3:

Pay special attention to places where the landscape changes from one type to another, like shoreline or the edge of a forest. Animals can be easier to notice in these places.

TOP TIP 4:

Make sure to wear dull colors and quiet fabrics so that you don't scare animals away with your outfit.

TOP TIP 5:

Try to stay downwind, meaning in a position so that the wind blows your scent away from the area you're observing. Many animals can easily smell you, especially if the wind blows your scent toward them!

TOP TIP 6:

Be patient! Prepare to sit still for what might be a loooong time, waiting for animals to feel comfortable about entering the area.

WHAT IF YOU FIND FOOTPRINTS (ALSO CALLED TRACKS)?

You're especially likely to see animal tracks in snow, packed-down sand, or mud. If you find tracks, here are some general questions that could give you a clue about what kind of animal it belongs to:

- How big would the animal that made it have to be?
- Does it look like a paw or a hoof made it?
- Does it have toes?
- Can you see claw marks? Can you see webbing?
- Do the front and the back tracks look the same?
- Does it look like just one animal made these tracks, or more than one?
- Does it look like the tracks were made in a hurry, or like the animal had time to put each foot down carefully?

Would going out into the field be tough or even impossible for you to do? Well... you could try bringing the animals to you, instead. You could make a bird feeder, bug hotel, or birdhouse. You could also plant some wildflowers in your garden (or even in a window flower box) to attract bees and butterflies.

You'll be helping the planet, too, by planting wildflowers that attract bees and butterflies. We know how important pollinators are. They're essential to plant survival, and those plants, in turn, are crucial for the wildlife that eat them. Preserving the balance of these ecosystems is good for biodiversity, and biodiversity is good for these ecosystems! It's one big, beautiful circle.

SIDE NOTE:

Plonk isn't entirely wrong to point out that bees and butterflies aren't the ONLY pollinators. Birds (especially hummingbirds) and animals do sometimes move pollen from plant to plant. Just not on the scale that bees and butterflies do!

Pollinators help humans in a more direct way, too – we need them to pollinate our crops! So it's a real head-scratcher to realize that we're also the biggest threat to bees, butterflies, and other pollinators. Our farming and the development of our cities have destroyed much of the wild habitat that pollinators need to survive. Our use of toxic chemicals to control pests and weeds often kills essential pollinators, too. The fossil fuels we burn are trapping heat and driving climate change that can confuse pollinators and cause them to become active at times of year when there isn't enough food for them to eat. Not much of a "thank you" to pollinators, huh?

YOU CAN HELP!

Letting garden space grow wild, not using pesticides, and growing plants that make a lot of nectar (what pollinators like bees and butterflies eat) are ways for you to support pollinators in your yard or neighborhood.

If you're getting a bit bored of your own local area, you could check online for webcams to spy on other people's! All around the world, zoos, aquariums, and wildlife preserves have cameras set up to observe animals, and anyone is allowed to stream them! You can watch cameras set up to observe watering holes, coral reefs, eagles' nests, bird feeders, popular animal crossings and migrations, and even a panda yard. Scientists can use these livestreams to observe animals without disturbing them, and to make sure the animals are safe.

You can also get involved with citizen science projects. Citizen science is when professional scientists get help from non-scientists to collect data and help them make observations. It's a great case of two – no three – no 1000 heads are better than one!

RECENT INTERESTING CITIZEN ANIMAL SCIENCE PROJECTS

EBIRD

eBird is a biodiversity citizen science project with hundreds of thousands of participants. It collects and sorts bird observation data and is free for anyone to use. Scientists can use the data for their work and birdwatchers can use it to find the most likely places to see certain birds.

Millions of bird sightings are logged on eBird each year. The data has been used for many purposes, from student projects to science papers to creating maps and helping conservationists monitor bird species and their habitats.

Conservationists can even use the data to make the case for new protected areas, based on the variety of species seen in a certain place.

ECLIPSE SOUNDSCAPES

NASA's Eclipse Soundscapes project called on the public to share their detailed observations of nature during the 2024 total solar eclipse, to study how animals might have been affected by the event. The project provided online training and guidance on the best ways to make observations and take field notes.

Did you notice anything strange about animal behavior during the eclipse? Some people noticed that animals started to do things that they'd normally only do at night. Some people noticed that animals seemed anxious or excited. But this anxiety and excitement could also have been the animals' reaction to what the people around them were doing – gathering and acting really excited about the solar eclipse. It's an important reminder to think about all possible explanations for a behavior instead of assigning a cause to an effect right away.

ANIMAL TRACKER APP

The Max Planck Institute of Animal Behavior has a number of citizen science projects to get involved in, including their Animal Tracker App. Scientists at the institute have access to tracking information about the movements of many animals. The technology is so advanced that they can tell where an animal is to within just a few meters of its location.

But these transmitters can't currently give them much more than location information and information about how fast the animals move. They're calling on citizen scientists to tell them what the animals are actually doing at these locations. Citizen scientists can upload their notes and photos to the app to be a part of the project.

The organization even has a separate Cat Tracker project people can sign up to join. Participants allow the researchers to track their cats and learn more about cat hunting behavior.

FROGWATCH USA

US-based Frogwatch asks citizen scientists to listen out for the breeding calls of frogs and toads in their local communities. All across the country, volunteers can send in their observations, usually made during a specific time slot in a specific wetland area. The organization provides lists of supplies and equipment that volunteers will need, as well as tips and training for monitoring the frogs.

Scientists use the data that volunteers turn in to learn about the frogs in different locations and to make recommendations about environmental protection and conservation of frog habitats.

MONARCH WATCH

Every year, monarch butterflies migrate thousands of miles from Canada to Mexico to hibernate from November to March. Citizen scientists participating in the long-running Monarch Watch project catch and attach lightweight tags to monarch butterflies along their migration route. As a tagged butterfly continues on its way, other volunteers catch and record its unique tag code. This data is added to the project database at the end of the migration season.

Volunteers may also create and register a "waystation", a place for monarch butterflies to stop, rest, and recharge on their long journey. Monarch caterpillars only eat one thing – a plant called milkweed – and it's often killed by chemicals used in agriculture. These waystations provide milkweed, flowers with the nectar butterflies eat, and shelter. Monarch butterflies are in decline and need all the help they can get!

Monarch butterflies have a useful adaptation: they taste bad to some predators because of the milkweed they eat as caterpillars. Their orange and black, flashy colors are partly warnings to those who might try to taste them anyway!

These are just a few of many, many citizen science animal behavior projects all around the world that you could get involved in. Have a look around to see what researchers need from citizens in your local area!

Lastly, if you have pets, you can definitely study them. Think about it: you've got a real-life animal living with you in your house! Of course, it's important to remember that tame animals are very different from wild ones, but you can still learn some really interesting things about animal behavior by observing your pets. Grab a notebook and watch what your pets do at different times of day. What things make them behave in unusual ways? For example, what happens when they see a wild animal out the window, or find a bug in the house? How do they act when it's almost time for dinner? See if you can answer Tinbergen's four big questions about your own pet's behavior.

DECODING PET BEHAVIOR

We've joked about having an app to give you a translation of your pet's language in real time, but there are actual ways to decode your pet's behavior. See if you can find your pet on the followng pages to get some tips about what some of their behaviors mean:

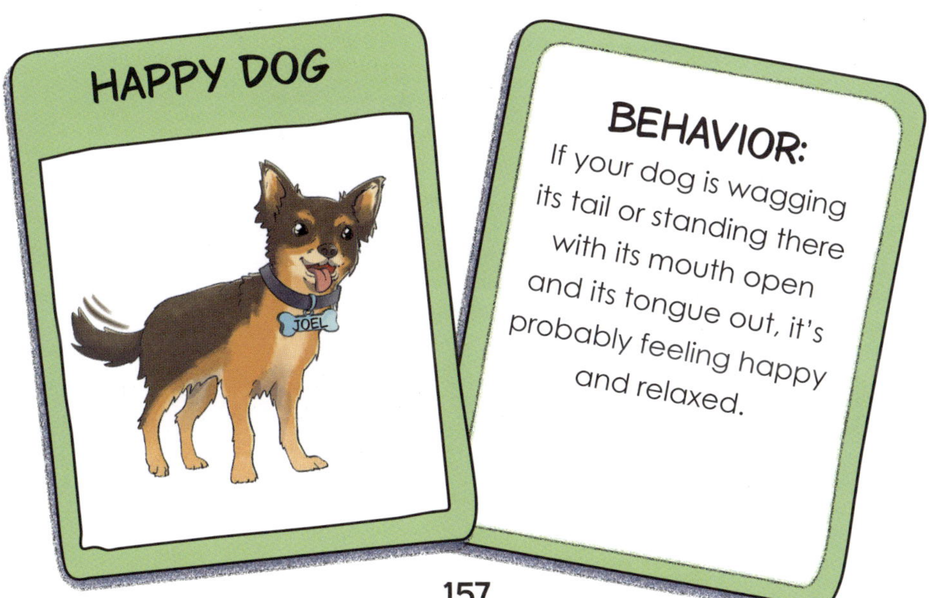

NERVOUS DOG

BEHAVIOR:

If it's shrinking down and trying to take up less space, tucking its tail between its legs, avoiding your eye contact, yawning and licking its lips, or holding its ears back against its head, it's probably feeling nervous.

ANGRY DOG

BEHAVIOR:

If it's tense, showing its teeth, making eye contact with wide eyes, growling, or holding its tail stiffly, there's a good chance it's feeling angry.

HAPPY/RELAXED CAT

BEHAVIOR:

If your cat's mouth is shut while it is stretched out or it has a relaxed but upright tail, your cat could be relaxed and happy.

BEHAVIOR:

If your cat is grooming more than usual, looks hunched, or stands sideways, it might be feeling slightly stressed or worried.

STRESSED OR WORRIED CAT

ANGRY CAT

BEHAVIOR:

If your cat arches its back, bares its teeth and hisses, or flicks its tail, these are signs it might be annoyed, angry, or ready to fight.

SCARED RABBIT

BEHAVIOR:

If your rabbit's ears are back against its head and its body is tense, or you can see the edge of its eyelid in the corner of its eye, your rabbit may be stressed or scared.

HAPPY RABBIT

BEHAVIOR:
If your rabbit is flopped on the floor or has straight but relaxed ears, it's probably feeling pretty relaxed and happy. It's also usually feeling happy if it's jumping and twisting or kicking in the air.

ANNOYED RABBIT

BEHAVIOR:
If your rabbit grunts or thumps its foot, it may be feeling angry or annoyed.

HAPPY BIRD

BEHAVIOR:
If your bird is making soft noises to itself, whistling, clicking its tongue, perching on one foot, or wagging its tail feathers, it may be feeling happy and safe.

You can even read some fish body language. For example, if your fish is hiding, it might mean it's a little bit stressed or shy. If you have more than one fish, and they chase each other, it's a sign of playfulness… or aggression!

Just like you watch and get to know your pets, your pets watch you! They can become conditioned to know what triggers certain behaviors in you. For example, your dog may hear your keys and run to the door, knowing you might take them with you.

You never know what you might see of the animal world from your own little perch. Keep your eyes and ears open and your mind curious. Watching animals and keeping up with animal science might even help you decide whether you want to study or work in animal science someday.

Chapter 8

WHAT'S NEXT FOR ANIMAL DETECTIVES?

There are lots of ways to become a professional animal detective. A fancier word for an animal detective is an ethologist, a scientist who studies animal behavior. Ethologists are often researchers, like the ones that have been the main focus of this book.

Ethologists are the original professional animal detectives, especially the ones who work in the field. These days, they often also work in university or laboratory settings. They might travel to spend lots of time in the field observing animals. They run experiments and field studies, usually focusing on just one type of animal or behavior for a long time. They might also look for lost species or for new species, or help figure out what effect human activities are having on animals. Their job might involve teaching and communicating their findings to non-scientists, as well as looking for funding in the form of grants or donations.

SPEAKING OF NEW SPECIES, JUST HOW OFTEN ARE THEY DISCOVERED?

It seems like something that would be pretty rare, but the answer is actually... all the time! Thousands of species (around 18,000, to be exact) are discovered, named, and described every year. But that doesn't mean they're completely "new" to Earth (though some of them do look a bit like they might have come from outer space!): they're just new to us. They've been here all along but we haven't noticed and documented them yet. They also can't make up for the species that are lost to the effects of human activity all the time.

Still, it's pretty exciting to think that about 80% of species haven't been identified and named by us yet, that there are mysterious animals all over the planet!

HERE ARE JUST A FEW SPECIES THAT HAVE BEEN DISCOVERED RECENTLY:

HYPEROLIUS UKAGURUENSIS

A new type of spiny-throated tree frog named after the Ukaguru mountains where it was found, especially hard to find because it is silent.

NEW COFFINFISH SPECIES

Coffinfish is a group of fish that can "walk" along the sea floor. This new species has big eyes and a very textured, red skin, it's one of 100 (!) new species found by a team of research scientists running a marine expedition with remotely operated vehicles, multibeam sonar, and other cutting-edge sensors, off the coast of Chile.

VENOMIUS TOMHARDYI
A new species of spider in Australia that researchers have named in honor of the Marvel character, Venom (played by Tom Hardy).

HYLOMYS MACARONG
A soft-furred hedgehog (with bristly fur instead of spines) discovered in Vietnam and with a name which means "vampire" in Vietnamese, because of its very long fangs.

If you do decide to study animal science, you don't have to be an ethologist.

HERE ARE JUST A FEW OF THE OTHER JOBS YOU COULD AIM TO HAVE SOMEDAY:

NATURE CONSERVATIONIST

Nature conservationists work to protect the environment. This can include keeping track of species and their habitats. Conservationists can work in the field doing research or organizing communities of people to help with environmental initiatives. They might also work in government, on planning and policies that protect natural resources and animal populations or manage land.

PROJECT: WHALE SHARK CONSERVATION

Someday you might work on a nature conservation project like the Whale Shark Conservation Project in India. This project works to protect whale sharks, giant, gentle sharks that were once hunted but are now protected by law.

WHAT DO THEY DO?

The project collects data on the sharks using photo identification, satellite tagging, and genetic analysis, and it engages the local community in helping to protect the sharks. It's a mix of science and public awareness campaigning, which is conservation in a nutshell!

ANIMAL NUTRITIONIST

An animal nutritionist is someone who's an expert on animal food and diet. They understand animal biology and the effect that the things an animal eats has on its body. They also understand chemistry and might work on researching food for livestock, pets, or zoo animals. Growing crops for animal feed has a huge impact on the environment. Maybe you could one day help find more sustainable ways of feeding domestic animals so that wild habitats are better protected.

ZOOKEEPER

Someone's got to make sure zoo animals are well taken care of! There's a wide range of responsibilities that come with being a zookeeper. Even though it's a job devoted to animals, it also involves working with a lot of different people, from visitors to veterinarians to nutritionists, zoo funders, and more. It's a zookeeper's job to make sure that the animals' living conditions are comfortable, that the animals are healthy and happy, that visitors are safely enjoying themselves, and that the right data is collected and shared about animal behavior.

Maybe one day you'll help run a project like the European Endangered Species breeding program at the Basel Zoo in Switzerland… or run night safaris at the Singapore Zoo… or run an animal rescue center like the one at the Australia Zoo.

VETERINARIAN

There are lots of different types of these animal doctors. Most veterinarians give animals check-ups and investigate why they might be ill, helping to cure them or heal their injuries. They may do operations or give advice about contagious diseases.

Veterinarians can work in small medical facilities or practices, in laboratories, at zoos, or in remote areas. They can even specialize in different kinds of animals (small or large animals, birds or livestock or cats or lizards or even bees, for example) or different types of medicine (focusing on anything from pain management to dentistry to parasites).

ANIMAL TRAINER

It really helps to understand animal behavior if you train animals for anything, whether they're pets, assistance animals, or film stars! Animals work in lots of different settings where they need to be really well-trained. It can take a lot of training to be a trainer, but it's an important job.

No matter what kind of job you have working with animals, the knowledge that scientists have gained about animal behavior will come in handy.

For animal scientists and researchers themselves, it's both a stressful and exciting time! Stressful, because these are people who are very passionate about animals, and they have a front row seat at what can be a pretty depressing show. The animal world is experiencing extreme losses. Every year, more species go extinct, at a speed that is unnaturally high and caused by human activities.

These include clearing animal habitats for agriculture, using harmful chemicals carelessly, hunting and fishing some species at unsustainable rates, and driving climate change by burning fossil fuels like oil and gas. Scientists estimate that up to a million species are currently threatened with extinction. It's sad to think that many of the beautiful animals we share our world with could soon be gone.

At the same time, it's an exciting moment for animal scientists, because there are so many new technologies to help them study animals.

HERE ARE JUST A FEW OF THE MOST PROMISING AND INTERESTING FUTURE DIRECTIONS FOR ANIMAL SCIENTISTS:

CLIMATE CHANGE AND BIODIVERSITY LOSS:

Climate change is one of the biggest challenges of our time, and it's urgent to study the effects that it's having on animals, ecosystems, and biodiversity. Whether it's keeping track of indicator species or using less invasive cameras and sensors to study hard-to-reach and sensitive species, there are lots of ways that animal scientists can unlock a brighter future for us all.

CAPTURING DRONE FOOTAGE OF NEVER-BEFORE-SEEN BEHAVIORS:

Drone technology gets better and better, and it's giving animal scientists access to little-observed animal activities. For example, one research team used drones to watch narwhals in the wild, and discovered the whales using their tusks to do all kinds of things they didn't know they used them for, including playing and exploring.

ANIMAL COMMUNICATION STUDIES FUELED BY AI:

As scientists gather more and more visual and audio data of animals communicating, and computing power continues to increase, we could be on the verge of lots of breakthroughs in our understanding of animals' language and emotions. Some scientists are even dreaming of one day being able to communicate with animals in some way by translating our own speech into language that they would understand.

THE CONSCIOUSNESS DEBATE:

Recent research and some of the latest thinking around animal behavior hints that more living things may be "conscious" than we thought. What does "conscious" mean, though? It's a really complicated question, and one that many thinkers in science and philosophy disagree about. Is it just the ability to feel? Does it mean an awareness of having a self? In any case, scientific studies of some animals are making scientists think twice. Evidence of the wide range of emotions displayed by octopuses, squid, and cuttlefish highlights the need for further research in this area.

Studies have shown that octopuses are amazingly good at solving problems. They can easily escape from different kinds of containers and their brains are connected in a way that leads scientists to believe they may understand and experience pain in a way many other animals don't.

But octopuses brains' are so different from ours that it becomes part of the challenge of deciding if they are conscious. We can't even imagine what it would be like to be them, and in this way the problem of consciousness is partly the limits of our own imagination!

BUT HOW ON EARTH DO YOU TEST SOMETHING LIKE CONSCIOUSNESS?

TEST

One test scientists use is to see if an animal knows that its reflection in a mirror is itself.

METHOD?

They can, for example, hide a mark somewhere on the animal's body that they will see in the mirror. If seeing it in the mirror makes them look for it on their body, scientists assume the animal understands that the image in the mirror is their own reflection.

Aside from humans, only a few animals do this: some primates (like gorillas, orangutans, and chimpanzees), dolphins, magpies, and elephants. These animals not only look for the hidden mark – they also use the mirror to look at parts of themselves that are usually hard to see!

How else do you think we could test consciousness? Maybe you'll help figure it out someday!

PET RESEARCH

There is a new rise in interest in researching pet cats and dogs. This area of animal research was pretty unpopular with scientists for a long time. After all, studying a creature that sleeps just a room away does seem quite a lot less exotic than trekking into the jungle to watch wild and more mysterious-seeming animals. But pet cats and dogs can tell us a lot about how animals think, learn, and behave, and they're a lot easier to access than jaguars and wolves. Plus, there's the fact that modern pet owners tend to be really interested in knowing more about their furriest friends.

Animal detectives have their work cut out for them. There are at least as many things to investigate as there are species on this planet! Whether it's in the field or in a lab, animal scientists use their powers of observation and experimentation, plus the latest cutting-edge technology, to learn everything they can about animal behavior.

As humans, it's pretty great to be the only type of animal that studies other animals, and that can use what it learns to help it understand its own effect on the planet (unless we have seriously underestimated crows, chimps, and dolphins) and to develop amazing tools and technologies. But it's also an awfully big responsibility.

Animal detectives can use what they learn to protect animals, protect the ecosystems that animals support, and protect their future (also: ours). They can even take inspiration from animal masterminds' most awesome adaptations and instincts to improve medicine, design more efficient vehicles and devices, and give our technology a powerful boost. They ask the big questions and they're prepared to be stumped (at least for a while) by the unexplainable.

There are probably dozens of animals going about their day all around you. Notice them! Start observing and gathering evidence. Let them inspire your very best new ideas. And remember how lucky we are to share a planet with these animal masterminds.

TOMORROW'S WORLD

Tomorrow's World is an exciting series that takes readers on an unforgettable journey into the core of the coolest sciences our world has **EVER** seen.

From the wonders of space and the depths of the oceans to the exciting possibilities of AI and the risks of an asteroid hitting Earth (gulp), this series is overflowing with fascinating facts and comic-style illustrations, showing how scientists around the world are constantly shaping (and saving) our future.

Written by renowned authors and reviewed by specialists in the field, each book is a perfect blend of fun, adventure, and of course, a fart joke or two.

This series inspires young readers to not just dream big, but to dream of tomorrow. **The future of science begins here!**

If you enjoyed this book,
check out some of the other titles in the series: